D0096876

SAM GIANCANA

The Rise and Fall of a Chicago Mobster

SAM GIANCANA

The Rise and Fall of a Chicago Mobster

SUSAN McNICOLL

ARCTURUS

PICTURE CREDITS

Mary Evans Picture Library: 14 (Everett Collection);

Getty: 24 (Chicago History Museum); 31 (Chicago History Museum); 39 (Chicago History Museum); 54 (Archive Photos); 62 (Hulton Archive); 82 (The LIFE Picture Collection); 83 (The LIFE Picture Collection); 89 (New York Daily News Archive); 98 (Hulton Archive); 99 (Archive Photos); 113 (Bettman); 117 (Bride Lane Library/Popperfoto); 132 (New York Daily News Archive); 142 (The LIFE Images Collection/Cecil Stoughton); 163 (Bettmann);

Shutterstock: 49 (Everett Historical);

Public domain: 106 (Chicago Tribune Archive); 122 (Press Association Images); 125 (U.S. News & World Report collection at the Library of Congress); 157 (Corbis Image); 178 (Chicago Tribune Archives); 183 (Chicago Tribune Archives);

ARCTURUS

This edition published in 2016 by Arcturus Publishing Limited
26/27 Bickels Yard, 151–153 Bermondsey Street,
London SE1 3HA

Copyright © 2016 Arcturus Holdings Limited/Susan McNicoll

All rights reserved. No part of this publication may be reproduced, stored in a retrieval system, or transmitted, in any form or by any means, electronic, mechanical, photocopying, recording or otherwise, without written permission in accordance with the provisions of the Copyright Act 1956 (as amended). Any person or persons who do any unauthorised act in relation to this publication may be liable to criminal prosecution and civil claims for damages.

ISBN: 978-1-78428-250-9
DA004722US

Printed in China

R0447476246

CONTENTS

ACKNOWLEDGMENTS

I am always thankful to the writers who came before me, leaving me a trail of history to follow in news clippings, magazine articles, and books. I hope my own words linger as long.

Special thanks to the librarians at the Vancouver Public Library, Central Branch, who enabled me to find a few missing pieces of information at the last minute.

To my late mother, Anne Caza, who located and purchased two hard-to-find books for me.

Thanks to Seema: Your help with chapter one and your skill in writing chapter titles are appreciated more than I can express.

Georgina Montgomery: I thank you for catching my errant throws and helping me to pitch a winning game.

And, as always, many thanks to all the cats in my life who have supported both me and my writing—you know who you are.

PROLOGUE

As Salvatore was dragged from his home by his father, he had no reason to believe that what followed would be any different from all the other times. The six-year-old was used to the beatings, which had become almost a daily occurrence since his mother's death four years earlier.

This time would be much worse.

An oak tree stood behind their two-story apartment and his father chained the small boy to the tree before beating him with a razor strap until he bled. The boy fell to his knees, begging his father to stop, but he was shown no mercy.

When Antonio Giancana's rage was spent, he went inside to have dinner, leaving his young son tied to the tree and facing the coming nightfall alone and in pain. He told his new wife of three years that he would beat the stubborn boy into submission. Finally released from his bonds later that night, Salvatore—or Mo as he was called by his father

An undated photo of Sam Giancana.

—was told to sleep in the corner of the kitchen. It became his permanent bed.

The beatings at the oak tree were gruesomely regular from then on, but, perversely, this abuse spawned in the boy a ferocious driving force. There was nothing he could not withstand, nothing he could not do.

And the world paid heavily for the man that boy became.

CHAPTER ONE
LIFE OF HARD KNOCKS IN "THE PATCH"

It was supposed to be the land of promise and opportunity, but it didn't look like it to Antonio Giancana when he arrived in Chicago. He'd left his life as a peddler in the Sicilian village of Castelvetrano and headed for the United States to make a new start. The trip had been grueling for the 24-year-old, becoming only slightly better when the Statue of Liberty came into view as the ship sailed into New York. The year was 1905.

Almost immediately the young man was on his way to Chicago.

As William Brashler described him in his book THE DON:

"Among the bodies that poured into the Polk Street station, smelling from days on the train and disinfectant of Ellis Island, Antonio was just another dark-eyed greaseball, a dago among dagos."

Antonio settled into one of the many crowded and dirty

tenement houses not far from Polk Street, in a district that had once been Chinatown. The area lay southwest of the Chicago "Loop," a small area bordered by Lake Street, Wabash Avenue, Van Buren Street, and Wells Street. On one side ran the Levee, a riverfront district consisting of row after row of brothels. While the Italians were beginning to overflow the tenements of Taylor and Mather streets, the Irish still ruled the area that Antonio had moved into and they wanted the newcomers to live only on the streets allotted to them. Over the following years, Little Italy—or "the Patch" as it became known—was born. By 1910, Chicago was home to 40,000 Italians. It was important for Antonio, as it was for all Italian immigrants, to stay in an area where he had many relatives and friends. They all took care of each other. Family was dominant.

Life in the early days of Little Italy was harsh. The tenement houses were not only extremely crowded, but often without heat, electricity, or adequate plumbing. Garbage was seldom picked up and disease was rampant. Horses that died in the Patch usually lay where they fell, sometimes for days, until city workers finally showed up to remove them. Meanwhile, stray dogs fought to eat the rotting corpses.

Despite these unsavory conditions, things began to look up for Antonio. He used his old skills as a peddler to make money, buying a cart and selling fruits and vegetables to his own people. It was not a fortune, but it was enough to get him to the next step in his dream. Antonio had left behind in Italy his beautiful and pregnant 19-year-old wife, Antonia DiSimone. Within a year of reaching Chicago, he had saved the money to send for her and their new child. Antonia arrived in December 1906 with their little girl, Lena, in tow.

The Giancana family moved into a walk-up flat at 223 South Aberdeen Street and Antonia went about doing what was expected of her. The women in the Patch had two main duties: to keep the house in order and to produce children as often as they could. The child mortality rate among Italian immigrants was very high, partly because of their living conditions and partly because of their insistence on using midwives only for all births.

It was into this environment that Momo Salvatore Giancana was born on May 28, 1908, beating the odds of survival even then. Shortly after "Mo" was born, the family moved into a larger home at 1127 West Van Buren Street. As tough an area as it sometimes was, the Patch also had an upside. It was an extension of the Old Country and the streets were filled with peddlers selling fruits, vegetables, pizzas, candy apples, popcorn, and the much-loved *lupine* and *ceci* beans. People sat around outside in groups, telling stories and drinking wine, much of it made in their own back rooms.

Although most of the children from the Patch ate very poorly and had little resistance to disease, young Mo and Lena managed to thrive, but tragedy soon changed that. In early March 1910, their mother developed severe abdominal cramping and began to bleed, signaling the beginning of a miscarriage. She was admitted to hospital, but there was nothing the doctors could do to help her. The day after her 24th birthday, Antonia died and little Mo—not yet two years old—lost his mother.

Antonio did not remain alone long. Within a year of his wife's death, he married Mary Leonardi. Together they went on to have six more children. But Antonio was not a happy man or a predictable one. According to his youngest son, Chuck Giancana, who co-wrote DOUBLE CROSS, Mo fell asleep at night listening to "Antonio's violent outbursts and the piteous cries of his battered stepmother." Mary was not the only one to bear the blows of Antonio's anger. From the time of his mother's death, Mo was beaten often and with increasing intensity by his father. By the time he was six, Antonio was chaining Mo to a tree outside their home and thrashing the little boy with a razor strap.

These brutal beatings at the tree continued throughout the four years Mo attended elementary school. Perhaps because of this treatment, Mo developed a defiance few adults knew how to control, and he was eventually expelled when he was ten and sent to St. Charles Reformatory for Boys. The reformatory, for "juvenile delinquents," had been set up to house troubled boys and steer them away from a life of crime (a goal it failed miserably to achieve, as witnessed by the number of its charges who later excelled in that area). Mo hated it there. After six months he escaped and returned to the Patch, but not to his father's home. Instead, he lived on the streets, sleeping wherever he could and stealing food. He stayed homeless and alone through 1919 and 1920, but finally found a "family" that would take him in: a gang.

Joey "Babe Ruth" Colaro was the leader. He was a stocky kid with big arms and a broad chest, and he reminded everyone of the baseball player, hence the nickname. Three years older than Mo, Colaro had acquired the street smarts necessary to lead the gang into increasingly serious crimes. While attending the same elementary school as Mo, Colaro and his friends learned to steal clothes from the lines in more affluent neighborhoods and sell them to people in the Patch. They quickly moved on to more profitable rackets. Their favorite was stealing "shorts," as they called unattended cars. The cars were then sold outright or stripped down for parts.

An alleyway in Little Italy, Chicago in 1910.

Colaro was always looking for recruits, and Mo jumped at the chance to join him. It gave him a new home and he was willing to do whatever it took to impress his new family. His greatest skill at the time was his prowess at the wheel of a car and he used this to make a name for himself. Mo raced dangerously through crowded streets, honing his abilities at "whipping" (taking corners at high speed), often on two wheels. He even set up an obstacle course on the streets of the Patch to perfect his talents.

Like all the gang members, Mo acquired a nickname. By the age of 13, he was dubbed "Mooney" because of his unpredictability and crazy, out-of-control behavior, alluding to people who supposedly go crazy at the time of a full moon. Those who first knew him at this time called him Mooney forever after, even years later when the rest of the world would come to know him as Sam (the Americanized version of Salvatore).

Soon the gang adopted a nickname, too. One night, sitting in Mary's Restaurant at the corner of Taylor and Bishop, a gang member told the others the story of Ali Baba, his brother Cassim, and the 40 thieves. They were impressed and decided to call themselves the "42 Gang," later shortened to "the 42s." While there was never that many members at once (death or prison kept their numbers down), the name stuck.

Gradually, they progressed from thefts to bombings and

murders. Otherwise they just hung out together and tested their individual mettle against each other. Mooney in particular was known to do anything for a dare. And by this time, his propensity for immense cruelty had begun to show itself. One of his pastimes was showing off new ways to bludgeon alley cats to death.

The "smartheads," as people started calling the gang members, inspired as much awe in the Patch as they did fear. The police in the area were all Irish and the residents felt they interfered in the Patch's affairs and never supported the Italians in any dispute. The community felt no loyalty toward the officers and was secretly pleased to watch the 42s outwit them. And when the smartheads couldn't outwit them, they bought them. Mooney was a valuable asset because a fast getaway from a crime scene was crucial. Failure to do so meant getting caught, and this resulted in having to pay someone off. The 42s had discovered there was not a "mick copper" or judge who could not be bought, but the price went up the closer any case got to trial. Colaro collected $10 a month from every gang member for the inevitable payoffs they needed.

MOONEY MOVES UP THE CRIME LADDER

The 42s were really just small-time hoods aspiring to be like the real "mobsters" of the day—the men who were part of the growing network of large-scale organized crime in the United States, which was known variously as the Mob, Mafia, or Syndicate. Such figures included the prostitute king, "Big Jim" Colosimo, his nephew-by-marriage Johnny Torrio, Giuseppe "Diamond Joe" Esposito, and Al Capone. Colosimo and Esposito were two of the most notorious "Black Handers" of their time, experts at using extortion methods imported from the Old Country. "*La Mano Nera*" (Italian for "the black hand") was a term that referred to a form of intimidation used to scare people into complying with a demand. The black hander would leave a note at someone's door demanding money. Such notes almost always said (in so many words) "pay up or be killed." The trademark imprint on the paper of a hand in black ink told the victim who was behind the extortion.

The big change for all the Italian gangs came in late 1919 with the enactment of the 18th Amendment:

"No person shall manufacture, sell, barter, transport, import, export, deliver, furnish or possess any intoxicating liquor except as authorized in this Act."

By midnight, January 17, 1920, the country was dry, but Esposito and other mobsters made sure that it lasted less than a second. Prohibition, which inspired bootlegging, did more to solidify the Mafia's beginnings in the United States than any other single factor.

As one of the biggest beer runners of the day, Esposito helped transport the better-quality alcohol making its way from liquor magnate Samuel Bronfman in Canada through Detroit and New York to Chicago. He then moved it from there to other parts of the country. His base was Chicago and the focal point the Patch, where a cheaper variety of alcohol was also produced. The operation of stills in hundreds of basements or back rooms in the Patch was overseen by the "Terrible Gennas," as the immigrants called the six Genna brothers who ruled with crucifixes in one hand and guns in the other. They were known as much for their brutality as for the hundreds of policemen they had in their back pockets. It all made for a trouble-free business.

Most of the Italian immigrants saw nothing wrong with operating a still for the Gennas, and those who did so wisely kept their mouths shut. They were also well paid for their trouble and made as much in a week as they could from a six-month job of hard labor. But the Genna brothers weren't the only ones to strike it rich. Esposito collected more than a million dollars a year from the Gennas' enterprise alone. The price everyone paid was the smell of "alky," which hung over the Patch all the time.

In 1923, Mooney made his first big move toward rising up the ladder. He got a job as one of the many strong young Sicilian men recruited by Esposito to collect the 300 gallons of whiskey produced weekly from each still in the Patch and deliver it in drums to warehouses across Chicago. Like the others, Mooney was squarely behind Esposito, often with the help of brass knuckles and guns.

Colosimo did not fare as well as Esposito. As far back as 1909, he'd begun having trouble with extortionists. He brought in Johnny Torrio from New York to help sort out the problem. Torrio, born in Italy but raised in the ghettoes of the Lower East Side, had become a busy man with a hand in many pies, including bookmaking, loan sharking, prostitution, and opium trafficking. By 1912, he was overseeing the brothels in Brooklyn's dockyard areas, where he sometimes employed a very young recruit named Alphonse Capone.

Torrio took care of Colosimo's difficulties quickly and efficiently, mainly through killing. In 1915, Colosimo asked Torrio to move to Chicago permanently to help run his prostitution business. Torrio accepted. Despite their success together over the next few years, Torrio saw the huge potential in Prohibition and tried to persuade Colosimo to move out of prostitution and into bootlegging. Colosimo wasn't interested. Torrio then brought 21-year-old Al Capone from New York to help sway Colosimo. When that still didn't work, Torrio realized there was nothing more he could do to change Colosimo's mind. So, he gave up and simply had Colosimo killed on May 11, 1920.

By this time, Torrio had opened up The Four Deuces, a dingy brothel and saloon at 2222 South Wabash Avenue. It was here that Capone, now Torrio's lieutenant, first met a young hood from the Patch he'd not soon forget. Recognizing Capone by his large size and the scar on his cheek, Mooney made a point of ingratiating himself with the man. It paid off. Soon Mooney was a frequent "wheelman" (driver) for Capone's hitman, Jack "Machine Gun" McGurn. (McGurn, listed as Vincent Gibaldi on his arrival at Ellis Island in 1906, later changed his name. He is best known as the mastermind behind Capone's now-legendary St. Valentine's Day Massacre, though he was never convicted of the crime. He subsequently fell out with Capone and later wound up the victim of a contract killing.)

"A good wheelman is hard to find, but a good wheelman with the smarts and guts to kill is a gold mine," McGurn reputedly said of Mooney to Capone.

Over the next few years, the two frequently worked together to eliminate Capone's problems but, in 1925, Mooney took on a major job for Capone in which McGurn wasn't involved.

The bootlegging operation set up by Torrio, into which he'd brought Capone, was moving along well. By the end of 1924, Capone was making as much as $5 million a year from it, but he still wanted more and he felt Torrio wasn't

Mobster James "Big Jim" Colosimo (left) with his lawyer Charles Erbstein in 1914. Colosimo built his illegal operations around prostitution, running a string of brothels in Chicago. He was murdered on May 11, 1920.

sharing enough of the wealth. With the encouragement of other Chicago mobsters, Capone decided his partner should step aside. Rather than use his own gang's enforcers (who might still be loyal to Torrio), Capone enlisted a couple of Esposito's toughs for the job. Mooney was one and Leonard "Needles" Gianola the other. They paid a visit to Torrio in January 1925 to tell him it was time to retire. Their message was delivered along with a number of shotgun blasts aimed directly at Torrio. He recovered from the wounds, but took the hint and left Chicago. The press blamed the incident on another gang. Mooney's stock rose again in Capone's eyes.

Next, Capone set his sights on driving out all six of the Genna brothers. Angelo and Mike Genna were the first to die in separate murders. Soon after, Tony Genna was gunned down—courtesy of Mooney and Gianola. The three remaining brothers high-tailed it out of town.

MO FACES DOWN HIS FATHER

Mooney's star was climbing rapidly in the underworld, but his luck soured in September 1925 when, now 17, he was arrested and convicted of auto theft. This led to the first of the four incarcerations he would serve in his life.

He used the 30 days at the penitentiary at Joliet, Illinois, to mull over his life thus far. As Chuck Giancana describes it:

"Sitting in the cell in Joliet gave him time to consider just how far he'd come since those days as a child when he'd been chained and beaten beneath the tree on West Van Buren."

When Mooney was released, he knew it was time to face down his father. He paid a visit to the family home.

By this time, Antonio had become relatively successful in the Patch. He was a partner in a small grocery store on West Taylor Street and the family lived nearby. Occasionally through the years, Antonio had caught Mooney breaking into the house to steal some food or find a place to sleep. Each time he'd beaten the boy and kicked him out. Not surprisingly, then, he wasn't happy to see Mooney walk through the door again. He screamed at the young man to leave, but Mooney just stared back and smiled. Antonio screamed some more and threatened to beat his son who, now standing at 5 ft. 9 in., was actually 4 in. taller than his father. Still, Antonio remained very strong and tough, and he was determined to rule his home like he'd always done—with brutality.

"Well, what do you want then?" he yelled at his son. "Tell me now and then just get out!"

"What I want is what you took away," replied Mooney. "It's over. You can't push me around anymore, old man. And you can't hurt me ... it's over."

Antonio still didn't get it. He lunged at Mooney in a fury. This time, however, Mooney was ready. He rammed Antonio against the wall and grabbed a large knife from the sink. With the knife blade next to the neck of the man who had so long abused him, Mooney threatened to kill him if he ever lifted a finger against him again.

"You would kill your own father?" Antonio gasped.

"Don't try me," was the reply.

From that moment on, Mooney became the boss and took over as the father figure to all the children. He became especially protective of his little brother Chuck, a commitment solidified when Chuck's mother was killed while pushing the four-year-old boy out of the path of an oncoming car. Mooney hadn't forgotten what it was like losing his own mother at a young age, so he pledged to take Chuck under his wing and look out for him in a way no one had done for him.

In July 1926, Mooney and two 42s were spotted by police after they broke into an expensive dress shop. A chase ensued until Mooney lost control of the getaway car and crashed. He managed to escape, but was arrested at his father's house the next day. Esposito bailed him out and Mooney was back on the streets—and soon back in trouble.

Although the sizzle of the Levee district of the Colosimo era had faded and many of its once-elegant brothels were closed, the district still buzzed, with small stores and clubs remaining open most of the night. September 13, 1926, was no exception. Summer was almost over and 18-year-old Mooney and a couple of his friends were bored. They decided to spice up the night with a heist. At 3 a.m., two taxis were parked near a small cigar store when a light-colored Chrysler pulled up in front. Diego Ricco and Joe Pape got out while Mooney remained with the car, the motor running. The store clerk, William Girard, was not paying attention to the well-dressed men until Ricco approached him at the counter and whipped out a gun. There was only $35 in the till, but Girard felt it worth defending and grabbed for his own gun under the counter. Pape was standing by the door and opened fire on Girard, hitting him three times.

As the shots rang out, the cab drivers ran to the shop. Standing out front was Mooney, who jumped into the Chrysler and roared away, but not before both the cab drivers and he all got a good look at each other. One of the drivers, William Jones, pulled a gun out from under his front seat and began firing at the two men emerging from the shop, who fired back. Both Ricco and Pape escaped down an alley, Pape with a serious shot to his shoulder. Ricco ran a couple of blocks away and flagged down another taxi. He told the driver, Alex Burba, to go to Polk and Racine streets. Once there, Ricco robbed the cabbie at gunpoint and then ran off into the street. Suddenly, a light-colored Chrysler squealed up and whisked Ricco away.

Following his instincts, Burba returned to where he had picked up his fare and found police cars everywhere. Through mug shots, he identified Ricco. The other cabbies picked out Pape and the Chrysler's driver, Mooney Giancana. All three men were arrested the next day and held on $25,000 bail, charged with robbery and attempted murder —which was amended to murder when Girard died in hospital. As he had done on other occasions, Esposito gave Mooney's father an envelope stuffed with money and Antonio went down to the police station to bail out his son.

The trial was scheduled for April 1927. The charges against Mooney in the earlier dress shop robbery were dropped for lack of evidence, but the murder charge held. In the weeks leading up to the trial, the three young men knew they had to do something about it. They tracked down Burba and gently asked him if he had had second thoughts about testifying. The 25-year-old, with a young wife and baby, was now out of the taxi business and owned a grocery store, living upstairs with his family. Although worried constantly, Burba refused to give in to the hoods, even when they offered him $2,000. Their last meeting was April 20 and Burba's partner in the store, Charles Ralce, later said that all the men seemed to be on good terms when Burba showed them out.

But that evening, Ricco walked back into Burba's store and asked for an ice cream soda. Sophia, Burba's wife, came downstairs and exchanged a few words with him. Ricco then asked Burba to accompany him outside so they could talk. It was 8:30 p.m. and dark, but Burba agreed. A minute later, two shots rang out. Sophia ran outside to find her husband lying face down with a bullet in his shoulder and another in the back of his head. He died in hospital an hour afterward. Sophia initially told detectives it was Diego Ricco who had come into the store, but she later recanted her statement. And in the end, she claimed she couldn't identify anyone: not Mooney in a line-up or Pape and Ricco in mug shots. Other witnesses also developed amnesia. As disgusted as they were, state attorneys had no choice but to drop the charges.

Mooney's world was good again. And it got even better in the fall of 1927 when his old gang leader from childhood, Joey "Babe Ruth" Colaro, was gunned down while stealing tires. Overnight, Mooney found himself head of the 42s. The stature of the self-proclaimed "Justice of the Peace" ("fixer" of things) went up another notch in the Patch. The new position didn't stop Mooney from continuing to drive for McGurn, however, because his sights were set clearly on career advancement in the Capone gang.

Esposito was unaware that the end of his reign was being

planned. What the 57-year-old also didn't know was that Mooney—the guy he'd found a place for and groomed—became part of the assassination plot. Instructions for a Capone hit had come to Mooney via Paul Ricca, another man who owed a great deal to Esposito. In a muffled message placed from a phone booth in Chesrow's Drugstore, Esposito heard the anonymous caller say, "Get outta town or get killed." He ignored the warning.

On the evening of March 21, 1928, Esposito was strolling down the sidewalk of South Oakley Avenue, his two bodyguards by his side. A black car began inching its way toward them along the curb and Esposito nodded at the passenger. Suddenly the driver (the best wheelman the Patch ever produced) put the car into overdrive. At that same moment, the bodyguards threw themselves to the pavement and hundreds of bullets ripped through Esposito's body.

From 1926 to 1928, Mooney was arrested on many minor charges, including larceny and disorderly conduct. Often he was found guilty and fined—and often he wasn't, thanks to rampant corruption. Politicians and the Mob, Mooney realized early on, were regularly in bed together. His early education in this began in April 1928 with politics in Chicago.

A group of men surround the casket of Chicago gangster Joe Esposito on the steps of his home at South Oakley Boulevard. He was assassinated on March 21, 1928

William Thompson was incumbent mayor and Capone's forces wanted it to remain that way. The main challenger for the position was reformer senator Charles Deneen. Thompson's man in the Twentieth Ward, Morris Eller, was being given a fight by Octavius Granady, the first African American to try to gain office in Chicago. On Election Day, the 42s worked as "floaters," traveling from precinct to precinct and voting over and over again. Many carried guns to threaten any election judge who questioned them. Mooney and the other 42s worked hard for Eller, but there was real concern that Granady might legitimately win. Mooney got the message to eliminate "the upstart, moolie, shine troublemaker." (Both "moolie" and "shine" were slang terms used as racial slurs against African Americans.)

Toward the end of the day, as he stood outside a polling station, Granady was shot. He managed to escape in his car, but was chased down and ended up crashing. The killer pumped 12 more bullets into him. A grand jury probe to find Granady's killers subpoenaed dozens of hoods, including Mooney, who was later released and never formally implicated in the murder. Morris Eller remained in power and Mooney's reputation as a killer swelled within the Capone family.

The boy from the Patch was on his way.

CHAPTER TWO
GRADUATION

The old days of using notes imprinted with a black hand in ink had given way to "pineapple" bombs as a means of extortion or intimidation. These small grenades, with surfaces like pineapples, went off so often in the Patch that residents hardly noticed them. One explosion, however, had more impact than most, especially inside the Giancana family. Antonio's store was continuing to succeed, having become well known for its Italian lemon ice, a sugary iced treat. On the night of September 16, 1928, Chuck was almost asleep when a loud blast shook him from his bed. He raced to the window and could just make out the glow of fire in the distance. Chuck saw his father outside, still dressed in his pajamas, racing toward the blaze. It turned out to be the store, where the front window had been blown out. Despite the damage, Antonio and his partner, Anthony Gremilda, were able to reopen in a few days.

Less than two weeks later the store was hit again. This blast ripped open the entire front of the building, blew a huge hole in the floor and broke the windows for half a block on either side of the store. The police questioned Antonio, suspecting he had ignored extortion attempts against him and Gremilda. Antonio insisted he had no idea why their business was being targeted.

But someone was bent on making a point. The night after the second blast, the two men were attacked as they emerged from their ruined store. Gremilda was shot three times, though not to the endangerment of his life, and Antonio was pistol-whipped. Still they stayed silent.

The authorities began to wonder if this was retaliation against Antonio's son—the man now known to police as Sam Giancana. Certainly, that was the word in the Patch, and the neighborhood became very tense because everyone knew this was one man you did not cross.

Chuck heard all the talk, too, and even though he was only five, he understood that it was just a matter of time before his brother sought revenge. "Mooney'll give the guy who bombed his father's store a good taste of his own medicine," Chuck heard another boy say.

And so, on a cool autumn day, Sam "Mooney" Giancana took revenge for his family—inadvertently in front of his little brother.

The five-year-old boy sat on the curb, holding a handful of small stones he was pretending were dice. He would throw them down in one go, then scoop them all up and start again. Although still very young, Chuck had already learned a great deal from watching life in the Patch. His education was about to take a giant leap forward.

At first he didn't pay much attention to the man who appeared and stood leaning against the lamppost. Then the man began to whistle. He was tall and, although the boy did not recognize him, he smiled anyway because the man was Italian.

"Hey kid, can anybody play?" he asked. Chuck shook his head in response. "This is a one-man game, but you can watch if you want."

"That's fair," the man said, continuing to watch and whistle. Chuck was retrieving his stones for the hundredth time when he suddenly spotted his brother Mooney out of the corner of his eye. Mooney was walking toward them very quickly and the boy didn't even get a chance to say hello before Mooney reached the stranger. There was a loud *pop* and the man fell to the ground.

"Blood gushed from his head like water from an open fire hydrant ... bursting in torrents onto the pavement," Chuck later recalled. "And then, as quickly as he'd appeared, Mooney was gone."

The boy stood there, paralyzed with shock. Pandemonium broke out around him. Shoppers rushed from the stores, barbershop customers still covered in shaving cream appeared, residents from the neighborhood called out from windows, police sirens screamed in the background. Still Chuck stood there, "mesmerized by the blood from the whistling man. It steamed in the cool autumn air." He hadn't realized there was so much blood in a person.

An "Irish copper" arrived and grabbed him by the shoulders and demanded to know if he'd seen who shot the man. Chuck caught sight of Mooney in the crowd a short distance away. His brother had already taught him about *omertà*, the vow of silence. "No, sir," he said, adding that he had been playing with his stones and had seen nothing. The policeman snorted in disbelief, but there was nothing he could do.

Chuck had learned his lessons well. The two brothers never spoke of the "incident" again, but Chuck would never forget the whistling man.

SAM MEETS HIS FUTURE WIFE

One consistent trait among mobsters was their ability to compartmentalize their lives. They could be cold-blooded killers during the day and family men at night. Their wives and families were totally separate from their business. Sam turned 20 in 1928 and so, like his cohorts, his thoughts began to turn toward settling down and having a family. He had "banged", as they said it in the Patch, hundreds of girls, but he was intent on finding an Italian virgin to marry. Her name was Angeline DeTolve, the youngest daughter of Francescantonio and Maria DeTolve. Angeline was small and slender and an early childhood bout of rheumatic fever had left her with a damaged heart. She met Sam when she was 18 and would talk with him in stores or at soda fountains. She liked him, but he would have an uphill battle with her parents because he was known to be one of those "crazy boys" in the 42s. There was no way her father would let her get involved with a hoodlum and he was very relieved when fate stepped in to divide Angeline and Sam.

Many of the 42s were now either dead, in prison, or physically crippled from their lives of crime, but Sam and his close associates were still going strong. In November 1928, Sam and two others decided to pull an old favorite and steal from a delivery van—only this time they decided to steal the van as well. They weren't counting on the driver commandeering a passerby's car and giving chase. The police noticed and pulled them all over. The three were arrested and released, but now they needed even more money for bonds and defense. They decided to break into a clothing store. Their ineptness again led to another arrest. With Diamond Joe Esposito dead and his father short on cash, it was a few days before Sam was released. His trial was scheduled for early in the coming year.

On February 14, 1929, the infamous St. Valentine's Day Massacre took place in which the goal was to kill Bugs Moran. Planned by Jack "Machine Gun" McGurn for Al Capone, the plan went off without a hitch except for one thing: Moran was not present. Although he often drove for McGurn, Sam was never implicated in the massacre. He told Chuck years later, however, that he had indeed been one of the killers that day. Just bravado? The truth will likely never be known because Sam liked to brag about "hits" the way a corporate president brags about mergers and takeovers. It was all about broadcasting power and status within the community.

When his trial for the van theft and burglary came up, prosecutors did not pursue the first charge because they had an airtight case for the second. Sam, feeling he would get a lighter sentence, pled guilty to the burglary and was given a stretch of five years in the state penitentiary at Joliet. He entered prison on March 12, 1929, only a few months before the Depression hit. It would be a very different Chicago to which he returned on Christmas Eve, 1932, for not only had the Depression made the financial picture bleak, but Al Capone had been sent to prison months before for tax evasion. Sam would have to prove himself to

The St. Valentine's Day Massacre, February 14, 1929. Seven members of Bugs Moran's gang were killed on the orders of Al Capone in a garage in Chicago.

someone new. The family he returned home to that Christmas was also in dire straits, for while Antonio had managed to start up his business again after the bombings, the Depression had hit him hard and he was forced to sell the store and return to peddling from a horse and cart.

Angeline had also not been idle while Sam was in prison. She had met and fallen in love with another Salvatore, nicknamed "Solly," and her father was very happy because he was a truck driver and not a "hoodlum" like Sam. What he didn't know was that Solly did his illegal activities at night and was one of Chicago's best jewel thieves. Sam knew this and, while in prison, had been kept abreast of Solly's activities and his blossoming relationship with Angeline. Not long before his release, he was told the couple had become engaged. Sam began planning his move: Angeline belonged with him.

Sam had been home only a week when he drove a black Ford out onto the streets of Chicago. The earlier snow and rain had made the road wet and mushy, and the blasts of wind and dropping temperatures that followed had covered everything with a treacherous glaze. Only the foolhardy were on the roads that New Year's Eve—and Solly and Sam were two of them. The Ford was on Solly's tail and it honked, startling the driver, who then watched the Ford's lights continuously flash off and on. Solly tried to swerve back and forth to escape the car and almost lost control a number of times. Each move was shadowed by the expert wheelman in the car behind, and then the Ford pulled up alongside Solly. He was struggling to see who the driver was and not looking ahead when he suddenly realized there was a sharp curve in the road in front of him and slammed on his brakes. The crash was over in an instant and, after slowing to confirm the occupant was dead or dying, the Ford disappeared into the night.

Angeline became emotionally crippled by the accident and retreated for months to her bedroom. Sam Giancana's greatest skill as he became older was his ability to read people. He would study someone to decide what they needed most—and then give it to them. Angeline was vulnerable and lonely and in need of someone to brighten her days with compliments and gifts. Sam waited two or three months and then began to pay her visits, much to her father's horror. It was not long before she was in love. She ignored the rumors that Sam was still seeing other women and they married on September 23, 1933. Throughout their marriage he saw other women frequently but he was very discreet about it.

While he didn't stay out of the business, Sam did manage to avoid the police during the next five years. He and Angeline moved into a small flat on South Hermitage Avenue, only a couple of doors away from his father's house. "Ange" as Sam called her, was told pregnancy would be difficult and risky but Sam was desperate for children. The doctors were correct and her first child was born two months prematurely on June 23, 1935. Ange recovered, but the child, Antoinette, was sickly. Eventually she was able to come home and Sam, by all accounts, became the doting father. Antoinette years later co-wrote a revealing biography, MAFIA PRINCESS, in which she talked about the conflicted relationship between herself and her father. Much like her father in temperament, had she been a son she would most likely have followed him into the Outfit, as the organization in Chicago was now called. As it was, Antoinette had a tough time coming to terms with the two sides she saw in Sam:

"For as long as I could remember there was a Jekyll and Hyde quality to my father's character and I often wondered how he managed to master such a dual life."

She continued:

"When I was a small child, Sam cuddled me in his arms, bounced me on his knee, and spent hours decorating our Christmas trees and putting toys together for me. And as he did those things ... he was also deciding whether men should live or die on the streets of Chicago."

The second child would come more easily for Ange, and Bonnie was born on April 29, 1938. Sam was a strict and demanding father—and husband. Ange was expected to be a dutiful wife, cooking and cleaning and meeting his every need. During the years of their marriage he often brought a group of his fellow Outfit members home for dinner with no notice. Ange was adept at having large pots of food on the stove to prepare for these eventualities.

Chuck spent a lot of time living with the newlyweds and it didn't take long for him to figure out that Sam had some hard and fast rules about marriage, including knocking Ange about when she crossed him. Most of the fights began when Sam headed out the door late at night and Ange assumed it was to see another woman. In truth, he saw other women all the time but when he went out at night it was because he'd had a call from Anthony (Tony) Accardo or Paul Ricca or Murray Humphreys. After every fight, Chuck wrote, Sam did something nice for Ange. He cared for her as much as he cared for anyone and he wanted a stable marriage. They went out frequently to movies and other events. Sam always made sure she had the finest of everything, that she had status among the other Mafia wives. She reveled in that and never left him. He could read people well.

In New York City, in January 1965, Sam Giancana leaves court after appearing before a federal Grand Jury in connection with a case concerning the bribery of federal officials and violence in interstate commerce.

DADDY GOES BACK TO COLLEGE

On December 5, 1933, the 21st Amendment to the U.S. Constitution was ratified, ending Prohibition. Prohibition had never stopped people from drinking. It merely handed the marketplace to the Mob, which would now turn its attention to other ways to fill its coffers. During the mid- to late 1930s, Sam cemented his place with those at the top of the Outfit. One of those was Paul "The Waiter" Ricca, who had come to the United States with a falsified passport while on the run from a murder charge in Italy. He went to work for Esposito in his Bella Napoli Café, where he acquired his nickname. He quickly moved up the chain of command, working for the Genna brothers and then Al Capone. When Capone was jailed in 1932, Frank Nitti was presented in the press as the head of the Outfit. In reality, Ricca became recognized as the man to see in Chicago. Sam was able to ingratiate himself with Ricca because of his skill at the wheel of a car. By the mid-1930s he was Ricca's chauffeur. He was also still the "Justice of the Peace" in the Patch and dispensed his brutal judgments from Louie's gas station at California and Lexington. Everyone knew where to find Sam. Some wanted money to back a business; many owed him money and were looking for more time. Sometimes he gave it to them, Chuck said, but most of the time he just gave one of his men "the look" and Chuck knew the man would be dead by morning.

Sam was a busy man for he also headed a group that continued to produce bootlegged whiskey, which was sold under established labels. After the years of Prohibition, the public never knew the difference. The Outfit was also heavily into the protection racket at this time and Sam was often summoned by Ricca to "persuade" a store owner that he needed their protection. Thanks to Murray Humphreys, the Mob had also moved in to take control of the labor unions, and Sam's persuasion was often needed in these areas as well. His form of persuasion was never gentle but it was always effective.

One of the largest undertakings in which he was involved during the 1930s led to another stint in the penitentiary. In June 1937, Guido Gentile, alias Joe Greco, found the perfect place for his group to set up a full-scale still. Belvidere was 110 miles away from the prying eyes of the Chicago police and while Prohibition was over, the demand for bootlegged whiskey was still high enough for big profits. Guido's partners in this new venture were from the Patch and included Albert Mancuso, better known as Sam Giancana. Within a few days he had found a barn and by fall they were turning out thousands of gallons of alcohol. Throughout 1938, production was at full tilt and so successful they had to find a storage barn somewhere between Chicago and Grand Prairie. They found one but were also drawing a lot of attention to themselves. On January 17, 1939, several agents of the Internal Revenue Service (IRS) surrounded the barn, broke down the doors and arrested everyone inside, including Giancana.

Again pleading guilty to get a lesser sentence, he received four years, and surrendered to U.S. marshals on October 16, 1939. He left behind a devastated family, one that was supported in his absence not only by Angeline's father but by Sam's friends within the Mob. Every week "Fat Leonard" Caifano, a lifelong friend of Sam, showed up with an envelope of cash. Antoinette was only four years old when her father left for prison and she was distraught.

"Doesn't daddy love me anymore?" she sobbed to her mother, who comforted her.

"Daddy's going to college," her mother explained to her. "Daddy's going to be gone for a while to learn new things."

Sam would learn well.

CHAPTER THREE
THE NUMBERS GAME

Sam wrote many letters to his two little girls from the Terre Haute penitentiary in Indiana. Antoinette was surprised to learn this years later when reading the FBI files on her father. She and her sister never received any letters and, as she recalls:

> "Bonnie was not much more than a baby and I could not read or write ... I realize now that those so-called letters were really instructions sent to my home and then passed on to [my father's] criminal associates."

Sam's first two years in prison passed before he met Billy Skidmore in March 1942. Skidmore was a hustler who had been operating in Chicago from before the time Sam was born. His skill was in playing both sides, greasing politicians and mobsters alike, and even playing gangsters from

Terre Haute penitentiary, Indiana, 1950s.

different gangs at the same time without ever bringing harm to himself. His boldest move was to collect $250 a week in protection money from the many gambling wheel operators in the black section of Chicago, giving a cut to Capone's group and then keeping the rest. What the wheel operators didn't know was that protection was not needed because Capone and his associates had absolutely no interest in them. Skidmore bought his way out of many indictments, but was eventually caught (like so many mobsters before him) for income tax evasion. This is how Skidmore wound up in Terre Haute. His vast knowledge of gambling and many other ventures was second to none, and he found a willing and eager pupil in Sam Giancana. It wasn't long before Eddie Jones showed up and so began Sam's graduate studies.

The simplest form of all gambling games was referred to as "policy." The name is believed to have come from the coded question that bet-takers asked prospective customers on the streets: "Would you like to take out an insurance policy?" The Outfit chose to call the game "numbers." The participant would pick three numbers (in those days, between 1 and 78) and place a nickel bet, or "gig." The payoff could be as high as $30, but was usually a lot less. (The game is similar to the Pick 3 lottery games popular around the United States today.) The method of determining the winning numbers varied, but the most common form in Chicago was the wheel—a large, crank-turned can. So many cans were needed that a factory opened in Chicago to produce them specifically for the numbers games. Wheel operators gave their games colorful names such as Calcutta-Green Dragon or Beans-Ham-Gravy because they knew that bettors believed certain games would be luckier for them than others.

The game began to flourish on Chicago's South Side at the turn of the century and by 1920 it was a major industry in the African American community. A large wheel employed as many as 75 people: runners who went to houses and shops, cashiers, guards, and wheelmen. While anyone *might* hit the jackpot with a nickel bet, the ones making the real money were the operators. In his book THE DON, William Brashler writes that some games took in as much as $3,500 and paid out only $30 on as few as three winning numbers. The earnings of wheel owners far surpassed what most of the Italian bootleggers were pulling in. Some owners were white, but most were African American —and of the latter, by far the most successful were the Jones brothers: Eddie, George, and McKissick.

The brothers were sons of the Reverend E. Jones, a Baptist minister from Vicksburg, Mississippi. The family had moved to Evanston, a northern suburb of Chicago, in the early 1900s. When Jones senior died, the boys' mother used an insurance policy to set them up in a taxi-cab business. But they saw a better way to earn a living. They drifted into "policy" running and, by 1929, had their own wheel. Led by Eddie, a graduate of Howard University, the trio became immensely popular. At the height of their success, the wheels were pulling in $25,000 daily. The brothers—known as the "Kings of Policy"—used the profits to buy legitimate businesses (such as the Ben Franklin department store on 47th Street) and numerous apartment buildings. They were all-powerful figures in Chicago, especially Eddie, in his expertly tailored business suits and white shirts. He lived liked royalty with his wife Lydia, a former beauty queen in the Cotton Club chorus. But Eddie was about more than just style: He was also a highly skilled businessman. Sam Giancana recognized it as soon as Billy Skidmore brought the two men together in prison—where Eddie was spending time for tax evasion. Sam sat and listened to him and didn't miss a word.

Later, Sam told Chuck that before he met Eddie Jones, he'd thought African Americans ("shines," he called them, in the vernacular of the day) were "stupid and lazy." Then he added:

> "But man, oh man, was I ever wrong. Chuck, there're shines on the South Side ... you wouldn't believe it ... shines who make millions."

Sam desperately wanted a part of that action.

If Eddie Jones had an Achilles heel, it was his association with whites. He used white management firms to run his real estate, even though African American options were available. He gave all his important financial business to white advisors and managers. He even made his payoffs to white politicians. On several occasions, Jones was criticized by other wheel operators for placing too much faith in his white friends, who enjoyed many visits to his home in Chicago and his villa in Mexico City. Still, he ignored the warnings and he ended up in Terre Haute, where he met Sam. More serious than that, he broke the unwritten law in the numbers community never to associate with members of the Outfit.

In the months they were incarcerated together, Eddie Jones taught Sam everything he knew about the numbers game. He even agreed to set Sam up in some type of racket once they left prison, with Skidmore being in for a third of the action as well. In fact, Skidmore and Sam had privately worked out a plan to take over black gaming in Chicago from Jones, but when Skidmore died of a heart attack in prison, Sam had a free road in front of him. "It's all so clear, Chuck," Sam told his brother:

> "Nobody in the Syndicate [Outfit] knows. Nobody. They never dreamed the colored bosses were rakin' so much in. Nobody knows … but me."

SAM FINDS MONEY IN MUSIC

Sam managed to shave a year off his time in Terre Haute and got home for Christmas 1942. Again, life on the outside had changed. For one thing, the country was now at war. Sam did his patriotic duty by registering for military service immediately, although he had no intention of actually going to war.

"I steal," he told the Selective Service official when asked what he did for a living, and he ranted and raved throughout his interview about all the horrible things he had done with the 42s. Not surprisingly, his assessment described him as a "constitutional psychopath with an inadequate personality manifested by strong anti-social trends." Sam found himself exempted from service.

"They thought I was crazy," Sam told *Chicago Tribune* reporter Sandy Smith in 1959, "but I wasn't. I was telling them the truth."

Now clear of army service, Sam next got a legitimate job —at least on paper. His FBI file reports him as working as a salesman for the Central Envelope & Lithograph Co. at $55 a week. His employer just happened to be his brother-in-law.

Meanwhile, Sam had cemented his position within the Outfit, where major changes were afoot. Its attempt to take over one of the fastest-growing unions in the country, the

International Alliance of Theatrical Stage Employees and Motion Picture Operators, had gone horribly wrong and the federal government brought indictments against Frank Nitti, Paul Ricca, John Roselli, and others. Nitti was ordered by his colleagues to take the blame. He chose to put a gun to his own head instead, leaving the others to ten-year prison sentences. Although Sam was losing his mentor, Ricca, he was quick to see another opportunity to step into the space created.

He met up with Eddie Jones's brother George, who had been given the green light by Eddie to bankroll Sam for $100,000—funds to help Sam branch out into the juke-box and records rackets. Eddie Jones hoped to have his juke-boxes installed in every tavern and club around Chicago. Shortly after meeting with George, Sam approached the brain trust of the Outfit. At the time, this consisted mainly of Tony "Big Tuna" Accardo, Jake "Greasy Thumbs" Guzik (who headed up the gambling operations), and Murray Humphreys. While they were not completely won over, they did give Sam the go-ahead to move forward with gambling ventures, such as the juke-boxes. They were pleasantly surprised when the juke-box racket brought in huge profits for the Outfit, which it continued to do for many years. Sam brought his friend Leonard "Fat Leonard" Caifano in as his partner in the juke-box business, and they quickly added vending and pinball machines. Then they brought another 42 gang member in to run the operation for them—Chuckie English. He took charge of the money skimming, done on a 50–50 basis with the store owner who provided space for the machines. The 12,000 machines produced millions of dollars in profits.

Sam was aware that he was rising up the Outfit's ranks a bit too quickly for the old guard and making them nervous. He needed one of them behind him 100 percent. In typical fashion, he chose a bold move to make it happen. In April 1944, Sam kidnapped Guzik and gave him a choice: take $200,000 to support him within the Outfit or take a bullet in the head. Guzik picked wisely.

By 1945, Sam had also become chauffeur to Accardo, who had taken over the day-to-day running of the Outfit after Ricca's imprisonment. In the same year, he bought a large bungalow at 1147 South Wenonah in the Chicago suburb of Oak Park, as well as the Boogie Woogie Club, a small saloon on Roosevelt near Paulina. His dream was to turn it into a Chicago version of New York's Cotton Club. Among the popular entertainers who played at the Boogie Woogie was Nat King Cole.

Sam added even more income to his ever-growing invest-ments through bootlegging enterprises he set up with some of his old cohorts from the 42s. And, war be damned, he made money counterfeiting, and selling gas and food-rationing stamps.

Eddie Jones, now out of prison, continued to ignore the warnings of his associates, particularly those coming from his close friend Teddy Roe, about staying away from Sam. He should have listened. Sam was given permission from the Outfit to take over Jones's operation in whatever way suited him.

"S—, I kinda like the guy," Sam told Chuck. "I don't want to take him out, but he won't move over and let us in. I gotta do something about him."

It was a day in early May 1946, a busy one for the Ben Franklin store, which had pulled in nearly $6,000 in cash. Jones, as usual, was there. He and his wife, Lydia, always drove the store's cashier home at the end of the day. Their limousine driver had just escorted the cashier to her foyer and returned to the car when two men raced across the street and yanked open the door on Jones's side of the car. He was staring at two men in long overcoats, their faces hidden by kerchiefs and two 12-inch sawed-off shotguns in their hands. They dragged Jones from the car, with Lydia clinging to his neck and screaming, and then hit him on the back of the head with one of the shotguns. In seconds, they had pulled him into the back of a getaway vehicle and, accompanied by a second car, sped off. Lydia's screaming had brought a police car. It gave chase, but when a volley of shots rained down on it from the backup car, injuring one of the officers, the pursuit ended.

The abduction made headlines in all the papers the following morning, but the Jones family was strangely silent.

Unknown to the police, the driver of the second car was Sam, and Jones had been spirited away to the basement of Sam's still-unoccupied new home in Oak Park. The ultimatum was clear: The Jones brothers could keep their South Side holdings, but the gaming wheels would all be taken over by the Outfit. It was strongly recommended that the family relocate to Mexico where Sam would send them a percentage of the return from the wheels. If Eddie Jones said no, he was dead.

Six days later, a $100,000 ransom was paid and Jones was released with tape over his eyes and cotton stuffed into his ears. He was glad to be alive and quickly moved his family far away. Sam now controlled all of Eddie Jones's wheels—impressing Accardo and the others mightily—and by August he had gained complete control of all of Chicago's numbers game. All, that is, except for one glaring exception: He hadn't been able to get those belonging to Jones's friend Roe.

Sam didn't want to kill Roe—so much so that he was uncharacteristically patient, opting instead to bide his time over the next five years trying to find a way to break the impasse. He sent Caifano to try to work out a partnership with him, but Roe refused. They bombed Roe's house, sent him threatening packages, and even offered him $250,000 to leave. Still, Roe refused to cave in. He became a hero in the African American community, and was dubbed the "Robin Hood of Policy." In truth, the Outfit was already pleased with the takeover of the numbers game and was not bothered about one holdout. But to Sam, Roe's resistance was a constant source of irritation and he finally decided to kidnap Roe and hold him until he capitulated. After all, it had worked with Eddie Jones.

Caifano was chosen to spearhead the plot to bring Roe into the fold. A gregarious, jovial man weighing 400 pounds, "Fat Leonard" Caifano had been a good friend of Sam's since their days in the 42s. He'd even played Santa Claus to Antoinette while her father was in prison.

On June 19, 1951, while riding in his car, Roe noticed the vehicle behind him flashing its lights. He pulled over and got out to face down what was coming.

"It's time," Caifano said to the two men with him (one of them his brother) as they all climbed out of their car. At exactly the same moment, Roe's three bodyguards (off-duty policemen) appeared out of nowhere and started shooting. Caifano took a slug in his temple. His partners, despite one also taking a hit, were able to leap back into the car. They sped off, leaving Caifano to die in a pool of blood. The bodyguards took off as well. When the police arrived, Roe said he'd killed Caifano in self-defense.

(Years later, when Antoinette heard of Caifano's death, she recalled her first Christmas when Sam was away in prison: "I guess for as long as I live I will never forget that moment or the fact that the man in the red suit was Fat Leonard. He had bought those skates for me. He had rented the red suit and played Santa Claus so that a little girl wouldn't lose her belief in Santa Claus. It is hard even now to realize that Fat Leonard was one of Sam's professional killers, a man who lived by the gun and eventually died by it.")

Sam was upset with the two men he'd sent with Caifano on the Roe job. One of his strictest rules stemming from his days with the 42s was: "Never, ever, leave one of your own behind." He let the two men live, but made sure they'd never move up in the Outfit.

The final act didn't transpire for a year, but it then came down quickly and brutally. On August 4, 1952, two men waited in a Chevrolet across from Roe's home. When he emerged at 10 p.m. and walked to his car, they ran up behind him and opened fire with shotguns. The force of the shots lifted Roe off his feet and into a tree before he ended up in the gutter. Because Roe had reported death threats he'd received from Sam to the police, Sam was brought in for questioning, but then released.

The bullets need not have been wasted. What Sam didn't know was that Roe had been diagnosed with terminal cancer and was not expected to live much longer anyway. This was apparently one of the reasons he'd dismissed his bodyguards and was walking boldly, unaccompanied, to his car.

"I'll say this, nigger or no nigger, that b— went out like a man," the FBI recorded Sam saying in the 1970s. "He had balls. It was a f—ing shame to kill him."

Thanks to Sam, the Outfit now held complete control of the numbers racket in the city. The Chicago Crime Commission estimated that, by 1954, the racket had netted some $150 million. Moreover, Sam was now second only to Accardo in running the Outfit.

However, 1954 was also the year that Sam's personal life took a couple of hits. On April 24, Angeline died of a blood clot. She was 43 years old. Politicians and members of the Mob descended en masse to pay respects and view her body.

"When Momma died, Sam walked around as if in a trance," Antoinette later wrote about her father, "tears welling in his eyes as he stared at her lying there in the casket ... he was constantly morose. He traveled frequently back and forth to Florida because that was where Momma died and the house held memories he did not want to shake."

After his wife's death, Sam turned over the daily responsibility of his family to her sister, Anna Tuminello, and her daughter and son-in-law. The three moved into his Oak Park home.

Then Sam's father, Antonio, died suddenly three months later. The upper echelons of the Outfit once again came together to pay their respects, meeting with Sam at Joe Corngold's cocktail lounge. The FBI was watching from a distance and worked hard to compile a list of the attendees.

Following his wife's death, Sam had begun work on a family mausoleum. He announced that his father's remains would be placed there too. Chuck took a trip out to the mausoleum one day to see how it was progressing and was surprised to find his brother there.

"Ever notice how the sunlight and the shadows make a cemetery look like rows of piano keys?" Sam said as he stared out across the graves, then continued:

"I noticed it when I first came out here ... when I did, well, I kinda realized somethin'. It's all one big f—ing game, Chuck. No matter what tune you play ... This is where you end up. Death—it's the great equalizer."

CHAPTER FOUR
VIEW FROM THE TOP

The early 1950s was a good period for Sam, who was continuing to intimidate, extort, and kill his way toward becoming the boss. But it was also a time when the Mob reluctantly began to find itself more and more in the spotlight. On January 5, 1950, U.S. senator Estes Kefauver introduced a resolution calling for a sweeping look at organized crime in America. The Kefauver Committee traveled to 15 cities to hold its hearings but its biggest appeal was that it was televised. By the time the committee finished, 86 percent of American households with televisions were watching. They came to know, first hand, the likes of Charles Fischetti, Jake Guzik, and Tony Accardo (the man Sam hoped eventually to replace as the head of the Outfit).

Accardo had come up the ranks quietly and effectively, working for the big boys (Al Capone, Frank Nitti, and Paul Ricca), killing as requested, and keeping his head low. As a boss, though, he knew his limitations and leaned on the intelligence of fellow members of the Outfit such as Ricca. Unlike other mobsters, Accardo did not hang out in clubs and keep company with prostitutes. Rather, he reportedly stayed faithful to his wife and spent a great deal of time at home with her and their children. He was respected as a boss, but not particularly well liked. Antoinette Giancana described him as "a rather simple and often crude and cheap individual." Still, Accardo's skill at running the show could not be denied. The Outfit under his regime had prospered more than any other organization of that time in the American criminal world.

Accardo's desire to escape notice by the authorities made him very unhappy to be called before the Kefauver Committee and exposed on television. He sat silent in his response to all 140 of the questions he was asked. Kefauver described Accardo, with his 200 pounds on a 5 ft. 9 in. frame and his thick hands and hairy knuckles, as "gorilla-like" in appearance.

Sam managed to completely avoid being subpoenaed by the committee. They could never find him.

In the fall of 1950, two potential Kefauver witnesses turned up dead and Kefauver moved quickly to ask J. Edgar Hoover, director of the FBI, to protect all his other witnesses. Hoover turned him down, saying that the FBI was "not empowered to perform guard duties." When Hoover himself appeared before Kefauver in the spring of 1951, his assessment of organized crime as being a purely local problem did little to help the committee's work.

The final conclusion of the Kefauver Committee was that a nationwide crime syndicate existed, controlled by the Italian Mafia. That pronouncement over, the spotlight on the Mob was turned off again and everyone got back to business as usual.

When Paul Ricca had been released from prison in 1947, he was pleased with Sam's work in his absence. Accardo, now the operating head of the Outfit, took over the wire services operation in the last years of the 1940s, with a great deal of help from Sam.

Wire services were initially set up to send news between the major newspapers across the United States. They became ripe pickings for the Mob, who liked the instant spread of sports information from coast to coast—and the fact that bookies could now take bets on horse races when they already knew the results: If they knew the horse bet on had lost, they'd accept the wager; and if the horse had won, they'd tell the bettor it was too late to place his bet. To have total control of at least one wire service, Accardo went one step further and set up his own service in 1946.

Estes Kefauver waves his hat to the press after the conclusion of the Kefauver Senate Crime Investigation Hearings, which took place in New York in 1951.

Tony Accardo, on trial for tax evasion, November 1960.

Sam had his fingers in as many pots as he could manage. His Boogie Woogie Club was doing well so he bought others. He also opened R & S Liquors and Windy City Sports enterprises, and still legally held down a job at his brother-in-law's envelope company. He even seemed to be involved in the food industry. A *Chicago Herald-American* report in 1952 said he was among several racketeers (Accardo was another) bribing state meat inspectors to pass horsemeat as beef. However, as was typical of so many other Mob-related scandals, this one simply faded away without even a trial.

Ever mindful of what had happened to Capone, Sam made sure to file his taxes every year, showing a healthy increase from legitimate sources. With the focus on Ricca and Accardo, the press paid little attention to Sam—that is, until March 1952, when a *Chicago Sun-Times* article named him as one of the "Bad 19," a list of Chicago criminals. All the usual suspects were on the list, but so were a few of the rising stars, Sam among them. Charges and indictments followed, but they failed to stick thanks to the rampant corruption on the political scene and within the police department. The only real threat to mobsters during this time came from the Internal Revenue Service (IRS), which watched them all closely. The FBI left them alone.

The Outfit's biggest move in the 1950s was into casino gambling outside Chicago. The organization's members invested heavily in hotel casinos in Havana, Cuba. At the same time, Sam and Accardo personally invested in the shrimp business, bankrolling a large number of boats and processing plants in Cuba and Mexico. Then, following the lead of the New York Mob, the Outfit moved on to Las Vegas. With a $1-million loan from the Teamsters Union Pension Fund in 1955, they renovated an old place on the Strip. The new Stardust Resort and Casino came to be owned by, among others, Ricca, Humphreys, Accardo, and Sam. By 1958, the latter two were each taking $300,000 a month out of Las Vegas.

Sam had reason to feel good as 1955 was drawing to a close. Accardo had been heavily scrutinized by the IRS and it was making him want to move out of the limelight—a spot Sam was more than happy to occupy. It wasn't long before the two men came to an agreement: Sam would run the show with Accardo staying on as an advisor.

Sam Giancana had finally reached his goal: top of the heap in the Outfit. On New Year's Eve, he held a formal party, inviting anyone who counted within the Outfit. Sam was in a particularly jovial mood—jovial enough to start a shaving-cream fight. His brother Chuck was at the party and reveled in the memory years later:

"The feds would never believe a story like that: Mooney Giancana, all-round fun guy. It was more like a fraternity

party than a Mob celebration: before it was over, Mooney had shaving cream all over his face and tux. Then the other men found more. Pretty soon, everybody was throwing champagne. It was wild, really wild."

Business, however, always won out over revelry in Sam's life, and a large part of that business was murder. In 1957, banker Leon Marcus found himself indicted for embezzling bank funds and he decided to use his relationship with Sam to escape conviction. He had handled many investments for Sam, including a $100,000 cash purchase of the River Road Motel in Rosemont in 1956. Giancana changed the name of the motel to The Thunderbolt, heavily renovated the place, and then had Chuck run it as a legitimate business. Marcus tried to blackmail Sam into fixing his upcoming trial, threatening to tell the IRS about the cash payment and a series of other investments. It was not a smart move.

"Seven out of ten times, when we hit a guy, we're wrong," Sam once said, "but the other three times we hit, we make up for it."

This would be one of the three "right times." Sam no longer needed to do any of the killing himself. Willie "Potatoes" Daddano was given the word and he in turn sent Sal Moretti not only to kill Marcus, but, more importantly, to retrieve the $100,000 cash bill of sale from the banker's wallet. On March 31, 1957, Moretti invited three friends along so they could "enjoy" watching him kill Marcus. The murder went smoothly, but Moretti made the fatal error of forgetting the bill of sale. He also left behind the cash and traveler's checks Marcus had had with him, thereby eliminating the possibility of robbery as a motive. The police quickly focused on the sales receipt bearing the name of Mr. Sam Giancana. The search began for Sam—reportedly last seen in church on the day of the murder. Always very adept at hiding from the authorities, Sam decided this time to allow the police to find him. In so doing, he managed to escape any fallout from Moretti's mistake.

Three days later, Sal Moretti was discovered in an abandoned vehicle. His body was in the trunk, stuffed into a dry-cleaning bag. There were deep gashes in his skull, burn marks on both wrists, and abrasions on both knees. He had also been shot four times, twice in the head. It took a few hours before police were able to identify the victim because all his pockets had been emptied and the labels on his clothing torn off. The only item remaining with Moretti's corpse was an aluminum comb, left behind as a warning to others to "comb clean" any crime scene or end up like Moretti.

Sam attended Moretti's wake with his daughter Antoinette, who didn't learn until years later, from FBI files, that Moretti had been murdered on her father's orders.

THE APALACHIN MEETING

On January 30, 1957, a Senate Committee, headed by Senator John McClellan, was set up to look into illegal activities within the unions. A young lawyer, Robert Kennedy, asked to become the chief counsel and arranged to have the McClellan Committee's hearings air live so that the entire country could learn about organized crime and understand its threat. A junior counsel on another government committee, Kennedy was, nevertheless, inexperienced and had little knowledge of organized labour. He would be a quick study.

On November 13, 1957, an undercover agent from the Federal Bureau of Narcotics, Joseph Amato, testified before the McClellan Committee about the existence of the Mafia: "We believe there does exist in the United States today," Amato told the committee, "a society loosely organized, for the specific purpose of smuggling narcotics and committing other crimes in the United States."

This was a major public revelation to Americans, and so dangerous for Amato that no pictures were allowed to be taken of him and he testified with his back to everyone but the committee members. An event the following day added fuel to the truth of Amato's words more than anyone could have planned.

Robert Kennedy (left) was chief investigator at the McClellan committee into racketeering. He is shown here in 1957, conferring with District Attorney Frank Hogan.

Apalachin, a small village just west of Binghamton, New York, was not a bustling town, and not the sort of place to see luxury cars of any kind. However, on November 14, 1957, state trooper Edgar Croswell was seeing far too many of them for his own comfort. He watched the many Lincolns and Cadillacs disappear into the rural estate of Joseph Barbara, a Canada Dry soft drink distributor, and thought of the background search he'd done on Barbara when he purchased the property. Croswell heard he carried a gun and a subsequent check revealed that Barbara had a Pennsylvania rap sheet with more than a dozen arrests, including two for murder. As with most mobsters, however, he had not been convicted.

Although suspicious, Croswell had no evidence to conduct a raid—but he did have authority to stop any vehicle on a public roadway and require its occupants to provide valid identification. With only one road leading to the Barbara estate, he decided to block it and wait for the guests to leave. He radioed for one backup car and three deputies. In the meantime, word reached the estate that something was afoot. Within seconds of receiving the alarm, mobsters flew out through the doors and windows, scattering in all directions. Some went for their cars and were caught in the roadblock. Many others made off through the woods and escaped. Sam was one of them.

"Well, I wasn't even gonna go originally ... but I did as a favor to [Meyer] Lansky and [Frank] Costello," Sam told Chuck. "I had to run like a f—ing rabbit through the goddamned woods. The place was full of briars ... I tore up a twelve-hundred-dollar suit on some barbed wire, ruined a new pair of shoes."

The Apalachin meeting had been attended by almost every top gun in the Mob, including all members of the Commission—the national board of Mob chiefs that came together from time to time to discuss issues that affected all parts of the country. When Sam replaced Accardo as head of the Outfit, he automatically became a member of the Commission. He'd wanted the meeting to take place in Chicago, but had been overruled. "This [Chicago] is the safest territory in the world for a meet," he'd later said to Stefano Magaddino, Buffalo's crime boss, when they were debriefing after the Apalachin debacle. Magaddino agreed with Sam, saying it wouldn't have happened if the meeting was in "your place."

"You're f—ing right it wouldn't," Sam replied. "We've got three towns outside Chicago with police chiefs in our pocket. We've got this territory locked up tight."

With the McClellan Committee hearings at full steam, the timing of the Apalachin bust couldn't have been worse. It only confirmed the country's worst fears: Whether it was called the Mafia, Mob, Outfit, Syndicate, or La Cosa Nostra (a name reportedly invented by Hoover and meaning "our thing"), no one could deny any longer the existence of organized crime. The Apalachin meeting also brought an immediate crackdown on all organized crime groups, especially the Outfit.

The press descended on Hoover with a million questions about who these men were, why they were meeting, and whether they were part of this "Mafia." Congressmen and senators were not far behind the press, but Hoover had no information to give them. Robert Kennedy even stormed into the FBI offices asking for dossiers on all 70 of the Apalachin attendees. Agents were able to produce only 30 files and those were sparsely filled, mostly with newspaper clippings. In contrast, when he visited the Federal Bureau of Narcotics, he was given comprehensive files on all of them.

Kennedy was disgusted. He said later, "The FBI did not know anything, really, about these people who were major gangsters in the United States."

CHAPTER FIVE
READING THE STARS

5

Sam Giancana wanted to be a star and Frank Sinatra wanted to be a member of the Mob. It was a match made in heaven.

"I would rather be a gangster than the president of the United States," a friend remembers Sinatra saying.

"Hollywood is just full of guys waiting to be used," Sam once told Chuck. "All anybody out there cares about is whether they're gonna be a star or not. We help them along and we own them. That's how simple it is."

Although Frank Sinatra's association with mobsters was not exposed publicly until 1947, he hung out with them almost from the beginning of his career. He was only 20 years old in 1935 when he was spotted by New Jersey mobster Willie Moretti, who recognized the young crooner's talent and quickly had him performing in casinos around the state. By 1939, Sinatra had signed on with trumpeter

Harry James, who subsequently released Sinatra from his contract when Sinatra was asked to join Tommy Dorsey and his band as lead singer.

Sinatra then signed a contract with Dorsey without thinking of the long-term implications. Under the agreement, Dorsey received a third of Sinatra's income, plus Dorsey's agent would get 10 percent on top of that. This meant that by the time Sinatra paid his own agent and union dues, he had virtually no money left. After a few hit records in the early 1940s, the young singer suddenly realized what he'd signed away.

In 1943, Sinatra offered Dorsey $75,000 to rip up the contract. He was turned down flat. And so Sinatra looked to his friends Moretti and company for advice. They obliged by paying Dorsey a visit. One story goes that they jammed the barrel of a gun into his mouth in their efforts to persuade him to release Sinatra (a version of events that Dorsey spent years denying; in 1951, however, he did acknowledge that he *had* been paid a visit to encourage him to let the singer go). Sinatra was soon a free agent again.

A few years later, the public came to know about Sinatra's socializing with members of the Mob, especially Lucky Luciano and the Fischetti brothers. He then spent the rest of his life denying he had a friendship with any of them. Nothing was ever definitively proved.

There's no question, however, that Sam Giancana and Sinatra met some time in the 1950s and began to spend a fair amount of time together. After Sam's wife, Angeline, died, he saw no need for discretion when it came to women. Sinatra was only too happy to introduce him to many young and beautiful starlets. Sinatra was also honoured that Sam always wore a gift that the singer had given to him—a sapphire pinky ring. Both men loved the fast life, but there was always more to it than that for Sam. He associated with most people simply for the good they could do him. Sam knew that Sinatra was close to the Kennedy family and this, Sam decided, was very, very good for him.

The "Rat Pack" began when Sinatra turned to four of his performer friends to create, unofficially, a small band of entertainers. The group consisted of Sinatra, Dean Martin, Joey Bishop, Sammy Davis Jr., and Peter Lawford, who just happened to be married to John Kennedy's sister, Pat. When one of the Rat Pack was scheduled to perform in Las Vegas, the rest of them often showed up for an impromptu show. Their performances were legendary and people flocked to Las Vegas to see them. The group was inseparable, filming, performing, and—especially—partying together. It was the latter that supposedly led to their nickname, given to them by actress Lauren Bacall when she saw them after a night on the town.

The "Rat Pack" in 1960: clockwise from left—Frank Sinatra, Dean Martin, Peter Lawford, Joey Bishop, with Sammy Davis Jr. in front.

Shirley MacLaine with Frank Sinatra and Dean Martin in a promotional image for Some Came Running, *released December 18, 1958.*

Sam became a regular Rat Pack guest and so too, at some point in the late 1950s, did John Kennedy. During this time, Sam also met Shirley MacLaine while she was filming *Some Came Running* with Sinatra and Martin. They adopted her into the group as well.

Of Sam, MacLaine wrote in her 1995 book, *My Lucky Stars*:

"I knew he was some kind of hood ... [but] I hadn't processed who Giancana really was. His face was the texture of dough and his dark eyes were recessed under lids like protective ridges."

They were playing poker together one evening and MacLaine kept losing, not realizing Sam was reading her cards from the reflection in the sunglasses she was wearing. A delivery came and when MacLaine put the food in the fridge, she noticed a toy water pistol on the first shelf.

"I pulled the pistol out and trained it on Sam. 'Don't I know you from somewhere?' I questioned, thinking of the wall of a post office. Sam leaped to his feet and pulled a .38 pistol, a real one, out of a holster inside his jacket. Just then, Frank and Dean walked in looking for something to eat. They saw Sam and me with guns trained on one another and fell down laughing."

Years later, another incident was not so amusing. As

MacLaine found out, Sam was an equal-opportunity psychopath who could turn from being very charming to get what he wanted from a woman to being exceedingly cruel to her for the same purpose.

The Rat Pack, she wrote, "took me everywhere, trailed by these friends who looked like gangsters. Giancana was recognized in some places; in others he went unnoticed. But when he was recognized it was with fear."

MacLaine was in Mexico in 1969 filming *Two Mules for Sister Sara,* and she traveled to Mexico City to see Sammy Davis Jr. perform in a club. Backstage, she saw Sam:

"He greeted me (God knows Sam Giancana was not an overtly warm individual) and I shook hands with him. His grip was strong. He glared out at me from under hooded lids. His shoulders were more stooped than usual.

"'Pasta?' he asked.

"'No thanks, Sam,' I answered. 'I've had dinner.'

"'It's good,' he continued. I sensed trouble immediately, maybe because he hadn't let go of my hand. 'I want you to have some.'

"'Oh, yeah?' I challenged. 'Well I *don't want* to have some.'"

At that, Sam grabbed MacLaine's arm and twisted it up behind her back, hurting her.

"Quit that," she told him. "I'm sure your pasta is *numero uno*, but I'm full."

His response was to twist her arm harder. At that moment, Davis came in and noticed the look of pain on her face.

"What the hell are you doing?" he asked Sam. MacLaine muttered that Giancana wanted her to eat his pasta.

Davis gently asked Sam to let MacLaine go. "She doesn't want any ... she's probably on a diet or something. You know how actresses can be."

Sam's response was to smile and then twist MacLaine's arm harder, causing her to groan.

At that point, "Sammy touched his arm," MacLaine wrote.

"'C'mon, Sam. Let go.' With that, Sam released my arm and slammed Sammy in the stomach with his fist. 'Okay,' he chuckled, 'no pasta for either of you.' Sammy doubled over. He had another show to do that night. I stepped back horrified. Giancana went to the bar and made himself a drink. Sammy straightened up, took a deep breath, and said to me, 'Why don't you come back later?'"

MacLaine left.

THE RAT PACK PERFORMS

Davis knew much better than MacLaine just how dangerous an adversary Sam was and that accepting a punch in the stomach was likely easier than any alternatives.

Years earlier, in 1962, Davis had been coerced into a month-long appearance at Sam's Villa Venice supper club just outside of Chicago. Sinatra had been guilty of letting Sam down badly. He had promised Sam that his influence with the Kennedys was strong enough not only to give Sam a hotline to the White House, but also to get the federal government and its agents off his back. Sinatra had failed to deliver on these promises and there would be a huge price to pay. Johnny Formosa, one of Sam's men in Las Vegas, had a solution.

"Let's hit him," he said of Sinatra. "I could whack out a couple of those guys. Lawford, that Martin pr—, and I could take the nigger and put his other eye out." (Davis had lost an eye in an automobile accident.)

Sam told Formosa he had other plans for Sinatra, but there was also another reason he'd decided to go easy on him.

"I guess I like the guy," he later told Chuck. "But if I didn't like him, you can be goddamned sure he'd be a dead man."

He may have liked Sinatra, but Sam still intended to collect on what he considered a debt. Repayment was going to require the appearance of many entertainers at one of his clubs, with the promise of huge financial rewards for him.

The Villa Venice was a clip joint in Wheeling, just north-west of Chicago, and in 1956 it was purchased by Alfred Meo, a Chicago restaurateur. (Clip joints were nightclubs where the patrons were overcharged—"clipped"—for very poor entertainment.) The true owner of the place, as almost everyone knew, was Sam Giancana. In 1961, the place changed hands again, this time going to Leo Olsen, another of Sam's front men. Olsen had grandiose plans for the Villa Venice and soon undertook major renovations for the express purpose, as he told everyone, of featuring big-name entertainers like those in Las Vegas. Sam, of course, already knew who those entertainers would be.

Sam also had another scheme for bringing in money. Two blocks away from the Villa Venice he set up a gambling casino in an army hut and he had a shuttle bus arranged to take patrons from the supper club to the casino.

In November 1962, everything was ready to go and a stellar line-up of Frank Sinatra, Eddie Fisher, Dean Martin, and Sammy Davis Jr. performed at the new Villa Venice. Each man did a solo act and, at the end of the evening, they came out on stage together to kibitz, sing, and generally get the audience clapping and cheering. It was everything Sam could have asked for, and the crowds happily took his shuttle bus to the casino and laid their dollars down.

The FBI was very interested in the Villa Venice and two agents later questioned the entertainers who appeared there. They all said they were working for free (though, according to Chuck, Sam had told him that each of the entertainers was paid $75,000 to appear). Fisher told the FBI agents he was doing the gig for his "good friend Frank Sinatra," and Sinatra said he was there as a favor to the club owner—his childhood friend Leo Olsen.

However, it was Sammy Davis Jr. who was the most forthcoming about why he gave up lucrative Las Vegas engagements to work in Wheeling.

"I have to say it's for my man Francis," he told the FBI men.

For Sinatra? he was asked. Or for friends of his?

"By all means," was Davis's indirect reply.

"Like Sam Giancana?"

"By all means," he replied again. He was asked to explain further.

"Baby, let me say this," Davis deadpanned. "I got one eye, and that one eye sees a lot of things that my brain tells me I shouldn't talk about. Because my brain says that, if I do, my one eye might not be seeing *anything* after a while."

As quickly as it opened, the Villa Venice closed down. It had served its purpose for Sam. Whether the entertainers were paid or not, he did well out of the deal. Between the Villa Venice and the casino, he had made more than $3 million.

Sinatra had paid off this debt to Sam, but his next one almost cost him his life.

Villa Venice was a small dinner club just outside of Chicago that was owned and operated by Sam Giancana in the early 1960s.

On July 13, 1960, the newspapers announced that Sinatra, Martin, Hank Sincola, and Skinny D'Amato had applied to take over the Cal-Neva Lodge and Casino, located in Crystal Bay on the Nevada side of Lake Tahoe. What wasn't reported was that Sam and the Outfit were in on the investment, too (a fact that reportedly caused Martin to pull out of the deal).

Sinatra was convinced the place could make money. To set the tone of it, he made the 1960 opening especially splashy, including on his guest list Marilyn Monroe, Joseph Kennedy, and Kennedy's son John. Also at the opening, but much less conspicuous, were Sam and fellow Outfit member Johnny Roselli. With Sam in Nevada's Black Book, he was officially unwelcome at all of the state's casinos—and any place entertaining him would lose its license.

In the summer of 1963, the McGuire Sisters were performing at the Cal-Neva, which meant Sam was there staying with his girlfriend at the time, Phyllis McGuire. One night, Sam got into a very public brawl with McGuire's road manager. The next day, the now ever-vigilant FBI handed in a report of the incident to the State of Nevada Gambling Control Board, along with photographs they'd taken of Sinatra and Sam golfing together. The ensuing investigation —punctuated with Sinatra having several screaming matches with the board's chairman—led not only to Sinatra closing the Cal-Neva on Labor Day 1963, but also to him losing his gambling license the following month. Sam, who kissed $465,000 goodbye because of the Cal-Neva closure, felt the way Sinatra had flown off the handle was at the root of the license being revoked. He was incensed with Sinatra and wanted the singer to pay him for the losses. When Sinatra balked, Sam—friend one moment, executioner the next—decided to put a hit out on him.

Cooler heads in the Outfit prevailed, however. No one wanted any more attention focused on the Mob than had already happened. Sam was persuaded to let the issue go and Sinatra, once again, escaped unscathed.

CHAPTER SIX
UNCLE SAM AND GIANCANA

6

In 1956, Joseph Kennedy found himself in a tight spot. He owed New York mobster Frank Costello a favor, but he was reluctant to pay up. So Kennedy turned to Chicago mayor Richard Daley, who owed *him* a favor. In turn, Daley contacted Sam Giancana, who did not owe anyone any favors.

Daley told Sam that Kennedy needed his help and asked him if he could meet with Kennedy on the East Coast. Sam replied that if Kennedy wanted a meeting, he would have to come to Chicago. Three days later, Joseph Kennedy sat in a suite in the windy city's Ambassador East Hotel facing Sam.

Kennedy explained that Costello wanted him to be a front man on a piece of property—in fact, that he expected it because Kennedy "owed him." Sam didn't understand the problem: Why wouldn't Kennedy just do what was asked?

"Look, I'm in a sensitive position given my son's political career," he said. "You understand?"

When Sam pointed out the obvious—the debt to Costello—Kennedy tried to make light of it, adding, "I haven't talked to him, hoping he would go away."

"*Go away?* You ignored the man?" Sam asked Kennedy incredulously.

"I can't afford the association right now," Kennedy replied. "And my son Jack can't afford the association right now either."

"You've insulted Frank Costello?!" Sam yelled at him. "How do you think he's going to react?"

"I already know. He has a contract out on me."

It was not Joseph Kennedy's first close call with the Mob. During the Prohibition era in Detroit, he had double-crossed the Mafia in a bootlegging deal and a contract had been put out on him then. That time he'd used his connections with the Purple Gang, runners for his illegal booze, to get the contract canceled.

This time Kennedy was coming to ask Sam to intercede on his behalf: to ask Costello to have the contract called off. Sam, of course, wanted to know what was in it for him. Kennedy talked about the day his son would become president.

Newly elected President John F. Kennedy with his father Joe on board a plane bound for New York in 1961.

"He'll be your man. I swear to that," he promised Sam:

"My son ... the president of the United States ... will owe you his father's life. He won't refuse you, ever. You have my word."

Sam chose to believe him (in spite of having told more than one person that "if there ever was a crook, it's Joe Kennedy"). In short order, Sam phoned Costello and persuaded him to call off the hit.

Sam was about to become a big player in two monumental events related to American politics. First, however, he had to deal with the fallout from the Apalachin meeting and the McClellan Committee, set up in 1957 to investigate illegal activities in the unions. Following the Apalachin debacle, the FBI's director, J. Edgar Hoover, had been embarrassed when the "there is no Mafia" comments he had been making for years were used to ridicule the FBI and himself. He was angry beyond belief and propelled his whole team into action. On November 27, 1957, he initiated the Top Hoodlum Program (THP), a large intelligence-gathering operation. The THP set out to target a number of hoodlums in each city (25 in New York, ten in Chicago, six to eight in other cities) and compile information on them. One of the young agents chosen for the Chicago program was William Roemer, who became Sam's true antagonist in the FBI, even though it was agent Ralph Hill and, later, Marshal Rutland who were actually assigned to cover Sam. From the very start, Roemer hated Sam with a passion and he spent the next seven years doing everything in his power to provoke the mobster. The intense pursuit of Sam and his colleagues by Roemer and other agents eventually produced more information about the Mob than Hoover had even hoped for.

The ten hoodlums in Chicago included Accardo, Ricca, Humphreys, and Giancana. When the THP started, Roemer later admitted, they hoped the chosen ten *might* include the leaders of the Outfit—at that time the authorities really had no idea who the leaders actually were.

LITTLE AL

The THP team worked on placing an FBI bug in a prime Mob location. They narrowed down their choices to the Armory Lounge, Sam's hangout, or the tailor shop where Humphreys conducted most of his business. In the end, because the Armory Lounge was often protected by police who were on Sam's payroll, the team decided to wire the tailor shop. They code-named the bugging device "Little Al" after Al Capone. The first transmission came through on July 29, 1959.

As Roemer later put it, "One microphone was worth a thousand agents." The FBI found out who was in power, what activities were going on, and which politicians were in the Outfit's back pocket. And, when they heard about an upcoming hit, they tried to warn the intended victim quickly and discreetly. They managed to keep the bugs under wraps, avoiding the electronic sweeps conducted by the ever-suspicious Humphreys by intercepting his orders and turning off the mikes. However, the mobster was never completely assured that his place was secure and he often opened his meetings with:

> *"Good morning, gentlemen and anyone listening. This is the nine o'clock meeting of the Chicago underworld."*

With the amount of valuable information going back to Hoover, the agents were quickly given the go-ahead for whatever they wanted. They did finally bug Sam's Armory Lounge, too, and learned more there than anywhere else. (The bugs stayed in place until Lyndon Johnson ordered their removal in 1965.)

A hearing of the McClellan Committee in August 1957. Senator John F. Kennedy sits at the center of the bench with his brother, Robert, just to the left.

The McClellan Committee was bringing increasing exposure to the Mob, but the person they wanted to question most was also the most elusive. Try as they may, they could not find Sam Giancana in order to serve him with papers. Only when he came out of hiding publicly during preparations for his daughter's wedding were they finally able to get him. It had taken two years.

On June 8, 1959, Sam finally sat down to face Robert and John Kennedy and the other members of the McClellan Committee. Given his agreement with Joseph Kennedy, Sam thought this was going to be short and sweet. He was not expecting the prolonged attack that followed. He was infuriated by this, but chose to keep his anger hidden. Wearing dark glasses and a toupee, Sam smirked and giggled through much of his appearance before the committee, invoking the Fifth Amendment plea (the option not to testify against himself; essentially, to say nothing) in response to any question put to him.

"Can you tell us," began one of Robert Kennedy's questions, "whether if you have any opposition from anybody, that you dispose of them by having them stuffed in a trunk —is that what you do, Mr. Giancana?"

"I decline to answer because I honestly believe my answer might tend to incriminate me," Sam replied, smiling.

All in all, he invoked the Fifth Amendment plea 34 times.

"Are you going to tell us anything or just giggle?" Robert Kennedy demanded of him at one point. "I thought only little girls giggled."

That comment particularly stung Sam, who felt Kennedy was trying to humiliate him. Nevertheless, with his long-term agenda in mind, he stayed silent behind his dark glasses. But, as he told Chuck later, he had another reason for laughing.

"Sittin' there, I couldn't help but laugh ... I was thinkin' about a night with his brother [John] at the Cal-Neva," Sam said. "It was all so funny ... I couldn't help it. What a bunch of f—ing hypocrites."

Still angry about having to appear before the McClellan Committee, Sam was not enthralled when he was then approached by Frank Sinatra on behalf of Joseph Kennedy, who wanted the Outfit to throw its considerable weight behind the election of John Kennedy for president. Sam wanted a show of faith and reportedly demanded that Joseph have Robert removed from the McClellan Committee. Joseph agreed, probably because he knew Robert was already leaving to run John's campaign for president.

It wasn't long after, in 1960, that Sam met Judith Exner.

Judith Campbell Exner [although she did not marry Dan Exner until 1975 she is usually referred to in any historical context as Judith Exner so that is the name the author has chosen to use here] was born in New York in 1934, later moving with her family to California. In 1952, she met and married the actor William Campbell. It was after her divorce in 1958 that she met, and very briefly bedded, Frank Sinatra. They were still friends when, on February 7, 1960, she was invited by Sinatra to a show of his in Las Vegas. Sinatra introduced her to John Kennedy that night, and within a month the 26-year-old had started what would become a two-and-a-half-year affair with him.

Less than three weeks later, Sinatra also introduced Exner to another powerful man—although she did not know it at the time.

"'Come here, Judy,' Sinatra said. 'I want you to meet a good friend of mine, Sam Flood','" Exner later recalled. The man in question took her hand and held it between his. "He was middle-aged, of medium build and ruddy complexion, but with penetrating dark eyes."

"You're far too beautiful to be wearing junk—excuse me —I mean costume jewelry," he said to her. "A beautiful girl like you should be wearing real pearls and diamonds and rubies."

"A girl like me does sometimes," Exner replied.

That was the end of her first meeting with Sam Giancana.

On another occasion, "Sam Flood" gave Exner one of his

business cards. One side said RETIRED in the middle. In each of the four corners was printed NO ADDRESS, NO PHONE, NO BUSINESS, and NO MONEY. On the reverse side was written "Under the Fifth Amendment to the Constitution of the United States, I respectfully decline to answer on the grounds that my answer may tend to incriminate me."

In April 1960, John Kennedy asked Exner to deliver a bag of money to Sam Flood. By then she knew who Sam Flood really was, but she had no idea that the money was supposedly to be used to help Kennedy get elected.

Help with the election was not the only thing an agency of the government wanted from Sam Giancana in 1960. Robert Maheu had joined the FBI in 1940 and had then set up his own investigative agency in 1947. His first steady client was the CIA.

"In the winter of 1959–60 ... the CIA still thought it could pull off the invasion [of Cuba]," Maheu wrote in his 1992 book, NEXT TO HUGHES. He added:

"But it thought the odds might be better if the plan went one step further—the murder of Fidel Castro. All the Company [CIA] needed was someone to do the dirty work for it. Professional killers. A gangland-style hit."

Judith Exner in 1960, the year she met John F. Kennedy.

The Mob had their own reasons for hating Castro, who had shut down all their gambling and prostitution operations in Cuba as soon as he came to power. All of Accardo and Sam's shrimp boats had also been lost.

Antoinette Giancana got to see first-hand the hatred her father felt for Castro. One day at home with Sam, she was reading the newspaper and casually remarked what a handsome and virile man Castro was. She added how she would have liked to meet him and spend some time with him if she wasn't married.

"Suddenly Sam leaped from his chair and almost instantaneously was at my side, ripping the paper from my hand and slapping my face," Antoinette later wrote. He yelled, "'Don't ever mention that b—'s name in this house again ... ever! That son of a b— ... do you have any idea what he's done to me ... to our friends?'"

He continued to rail at her and pound the table before screaming, "Get outta here before I kill you." She did.

The CIA contacted Maheu to organize and arrange what was, undeniably, a hit. "I knew that the CIA was talking about murder," Maheu said. At first reluctant, eventually he agreed. When he offered the contract to Johnny Roselli, the mobster began to laugh.

"Me? You want *me* to get involved with Uncle Sam?" he asked Maheu. "The Feds are tailing me wherever I go ...

They're always trying to get something on me. Bob, are you sure you're talking to the right guy?"

Roselli did not have the authority to agree to something of this nature, so he arranged for a meeting in Miami on October 11, 1960 between Maheu and two men he introduced as Sam Gold and Joe. Sam Gold was Sam Giancana, who was to be Roselli's backup man, and Joe was Santo Trafficante Jr., who was to be the direct contact in Cuba. Maheu had no idea at the time that Sam was the head of the Mafia in Chicago and Trafficante the Syndicate chief in Florida. He told them the CIA was willing to pay $150,000 to have Castro killed.

When methods came up in the discussion, Sam advised using something like poison rather than a bullet to the head.

"He said that no one could be recruited to do the job [firing at close range], because the chance of survival and escape would be negligible," stated a 1967 report on the Castro plot, prepared by the CIA's inspector-general.

On March 12, 1961, a CIA operative met with the three mobsters and handed over poison pills and a down payment of $10,000. In all, the CIA reportedly spent $100,000 on the operation and Sam used $90,000 of the Mob's own money to cover expenses. Plans, however, had to be shelved after the failed April 1961 Bay of Pigs invasion by U.S. troops.

Fidel Castro, the president of Cuba, in 1959

Many sources have stated that both John and Robert Kennedy knew about the plot to assassinate Castro. In early 1962, Robert discovered that the CIA was trying to protect Sam Giancana from prosecution on another matter. When pushed, the agency confessed about Sam's involvement in the murder plot against Castro.

"I trust that if you ever try to do business with organized crime again—with gangsters—you will let the attorney general know," Kennedy is said to have told the CIA official.

Meanwhile, John Kennedy had apparently been sending messages to Sam through Exner.

"He didn't trust the CIA to eliminate Castro," she told syndicated newspaper columnist Liz Smith, "and he decided to deal with the Mob himself. Jack had good instincts about people. He knew the ones he could trust … Jack told me he [Sam] was 'working with us' against Castro, so I never considered Sam to be an ogre!"

As for helping to ensure John Kennedy was elected president, Sam and his team worked very hard from the primaries on. An FBI wiretap later recorded Sam and Roselli discussing the "donations" they had made. His men were also out in full force to ensure all members of the unions voted in favor of Kennedy, and they spread a great deal of money around to make it happen. The Outfit was convinced that if they did this, the future Kennedy administration would owe them.

The election was incredibly close and the State of Illinois, as it turned out, was crucial. This played right into Sam's hands. When the results were in on November 8, 1960, John Kennedy was president of the United States, but only by the tiniest of margins. Sam was not the only mobster behind the victory, but he was convinced that he alone was responsible for it.

"Listen, honey," Sam told Exner. "If it wasn't for me, your boyfriend wouldn't even be in the White House."

Sam had long believed the big payoff was just around the corner. But by the time Joe Valachi broke the vow of *omertà* and testified against the Mob (in front of another McClellan Committee looking into Mob structure and activities) in 1963, Sam had come to understand there would be no such payoff. Although Valachi's testimony hurt the New York Mafia much more than the Outfit in Chicago, Sam was pleased there was a $100,000 price on the head of the mobster everyone called two-faced. And he had come to feel much the same way about Joseph Kennedy.

Valachi's closing words to Congress on the last day he testified were clear but ominous:

"Gentlemen, I'll say this. Some day the Mob is going to put a man in the White House, and he's not going to know it until they present him with the bill."

CHAPTER SEVEN
BETRAYAL

"**A**ren't they hypocritical?" Santo Trafficante Jr., Florida crime boss, said to an associate. "Here's this guy, Bobby Kennedy, talking about law and order, and these guys made their goddamn fortune through bootlegging. Bobby Kennedy is stepping on too many toes ... you wait and see, somebody is going to kill those sons-of-bitches. It's just a matter of time."

Sam was also beyond angry.

"If I was gonna get f—ed, at least it shoulda felt good," Sam told Chuck.

The three years since the election had shown all members of the Mob across the U.S. that the Kennedys were out to get them. In exchange for their election support, Joseph Kennedy had told New York's Bonanno crime family that Robert would be named ambassador "to Ireland or something like that." It was therefore a shock to them and to the

Santo Trafficante (right) leaves the Criminal Court in New York with his attorney Frank Ragano after appearing before a Grand Jury.

members of the Outfit when, shortly after taking office, John Kennedy named his brother as the country's new Attorney General. The FBI crackdown initiated in 1957 would most likely have faded away had Robert Kennedy not been given the position. The FBI's J. Edgar Hoover was reportedly no happier than the Mob about the appointment.

Robert quickly made his agenda very clear: It was time to go after the Mob. As he wrote in his book, THE ENEMY WITHIN:

> *"If we do not on a national scale attack organized criminals with weapons and techniques as effective as their own, they will destroy us."*

Robert put pressure on the FBI to step up its surveillance and attacks on the Mob in general and Sam Giancana in particular.

It may have made Sam angry, but it did not stop his efforts to expand his empire. One potential conquest was the Dominican Republic. With FBI agents William Roemer and Marshall Rutland listening in, Sam talked about establishing a "gambling stronghold" in the island nation. Sam himself even made a trip to the capital Santo Domingo in May 1963 to see how negotiations on his behalf were going. No deal was struck then, and a civil war in the country soon after derailed the plans for good.

Still, Roemer's early concern over Sam's move into the Dominican Republic was that it would give him more funds to corrupt Chicago officials. Roemer felt that if the FBI stepped up their surveillance of Sam, maybe they could hamper his plans. Rutland, the agent officially assigned to keep an eye on Sam, went to his superiors and received approval for what became known as "lockstep." This meant that from the second Sam woke up in the morning to the second he went to bed at night agents would stay only a couple of feet away from him, every day. Roemer was in charge of putting the program into action and he couldn't wait.

"I won't deny that part of my scheme was to make life miserable for the guy I now considered my arch enemy," Roemer later recounted.

And he worked hard at doing just that. Unfortunately, his enthusiasm backfired on him. The first time Sam went for a walk and Roemer followed, the agent couldn't help badgering him.

"I said that he should just get out of the country. I said that nobody wanted him around, not even his own people."

It was inappropriate behavior for an FBI agent

For six weeks, lockstep continued and so did the verbal taunts. Even on the golf course, the agents stayed right behind Sam, teeing off on the same hole where Sam was trying to make his second shot. Finally Sam went on the attack, using a movie camera to film the agents following him to church (suddenly one of his regular destinations), to the cemetery, on the golf course—everywhere. But while other agents hid from the camera, Roemer stared boldly back.

"Giancana sues the FBI," the newspaper headlines soon read. "Mob boss says the FBI 'harassing me'."

It was classic Sam and he was in his element in court. His lawyers had the film footage and documentation of the comments Roemer had made. Even Sam's old Aunt Rose took the stand to say the FBI had harassed her and that she was "terrified." When Sam was called to testify, opening himself up to questions about his criminal activities, Roemer was shocked when no cross-examination ensued. As he later learned, the U.S. attorney handling the case had his orders—from Robert Kennedy no less—not to cross-examine Sam. And this held, apparently even after the following exchange took place during the hearing:

"Were you, Sam Giancana, guilty of breaking any local, state, or federal law that could warrant such FBI surveillance?" asked the prosecutor.

Sam looked him straight in the eye and answered, "No."

If lack of legal backup wasn't demoralizing enough to the agents, one of them was fined $500 for contempt of court for refusing to answer questions about the surveillance. Sam won the case and the right to have the FBI's surveillance of him restricted. The ruling was subsequently overturned, but the initial victory made the FBI look foolish.

Meanwhile, Sam was still hanging out with Sinatra, John (Jack) Kennedy, and Judith Exner. His "friendship" with Kennedy notwithstanding, Sam was also busy compiling a dossier on the married president's sexual conquests and exploits. For Sam, such record-keeping was a hedge against the future.

Kennedy's affair with Exner was the most serious of all his dalliances. He was obsessed with her and worried she was seeing other men. She wasn't. She was totally in love with him, as she confessed to author Seymour Hersh in The Dark Side of Camelot:

> "I knew this was something I should stay away from, but my heart started ruling my head. I can't make any excuses for it."

The last meeting she knew of between Sam and Jack was on August 8, 1961. In later years, experts looked at all the phone numbers and dates she provided and everything she said about her relationship with Jack checked out. They also confirmed that Jack and Sam were both in the same town when Exner said meetings had taken place between them.

Exner's heart was putting her in a treacherous position.

In addition to running messages between Kennedy and Sam, she also found herself occasionally doing the same thing for Kennedy and other parties. In 1962, for example, Exner —at Kennedy's request—brought payoffs to him from a group of California businessmen interested in obtaining defense contracts. Asked during a subsequent interview with columnist Liz Smith how she felt about being a go-between, Exner replied, "I was 26 and in love. Was I supposed to have better sense and judgment than the president of the United States?"

This and other facts about her affair might never have come to light had she not been called to testify before the 1975 Senate Church Committee looking into assassination plots, notably the ones against Fidel Castro. The committee wanted to know if either Sam Giancana or Johnny Roselli had ever asked her to communicate messages to, or set up meetings with, the president. Exner answered, "No," which was not exactly a lie but also not the total truth either. Much later she admitted it was actually President Kennedy who had set up the meetings and communications—that he was always the instigator.

In front of the committee, she freely acknowledged the affair, but held back many of the details and lied about others. Many lies even crept into her 1977 book, My Story, as she eventually confessed to Smith in a 1997 interview.

One of those untruths was that she had had affairs with Kennedy and Sam simultaneously. She was afraid to tell the truth about everything, she told Smith, because she was terrified for her life and increasingly aware of the danger of her situation:

"All those years, I was so scared of being killed ... I still sleep with a gun under my pillow after all this time."

Exner was told her testimony before the Senate Church Committee would be confidential, but in no time her name and the details of her affair were leaked to the press. From that moment on, her entire life was open for all to scrutinize.

By 1962, problems were plaguing Exner's relationship with Kennedy. With the FBI constantly harassing her, John wanted her to move to Washington so he could be close to her and protect her. At the same time, she was feeling more and more anguish about being the "other woman."

Then, on March 22, 1962, Hoover had lunch with Kennedy, who had already been warned by his brother what the topic of conversation would be. Hoover told Kennedy that he knew about his affair and informed him about Exner's ties to Sam Giancana and Johnny Roselli, pretending that the president did not know this, even though Hoover knew he did. The message from Hoover was clear: End the relationship.

Kennedy said he would, but the calls between him and Exner still carried on for months after that (as White House phone logs confirm). Nevertheless, the affair did slowly start to wind down and Exner was the one to finally end it.

"Jack begged me to come back and talk, to try again," she told Liz Smith. And she did do just that, one final time, in December 1962, but she let Kennedy know she wouldn't see him again after that because it was too painful. "But we were intimate that one last time, in the White House. I still loved him with all my heart."

Two months later, Exner realized she was pregnant. She'd had some gynecological problems and thought she couldn't get pregnant. "I was stunned. I hadn't been with anyone but Jack—*not ever during the whole time.*"

She phoned Kennedy to tell him. He asked if she wanted to keep the baby and said that, if so, it could be arranged. "That's an absolute impossibility because of who you are, and we'd never get away with it," she told him. They then discussed abortion, which was still illegal at that time.

"Jack said, 'Do you think Sam would help us? Would you ask Sam?'"

Over dinner with Sam soon after that, Exner told him what had happened.

"Damn him! Damn that Kennedy!" was his first response.

Sam told Exner he would arrange anything she wanted —and that if she wanted to keep the baby, she could do that too. And then he leaned forward and took her hands in his. "Let me ask you this: Will you marry me?"

She was so taken aback, she burst into tears. "I was so touched by Sam. It broke me down."

Exner knew Sam was in love with the singer Phyllis McGuire and told him, "Sam, you don't want to marry me."

"Yes, maybe, but you deserve to be asked," he replied.

"There are a lot of things that they can say about Sam," she later said to Smith, "but no one can ever take that away from me—that moment when he tried to make it right." That night, Exner and Sam "were intimate," the one and only time.

Shortly afterward, Exner had an abortion at Chicago's Grant Hospital (she supplied the receipts and the name of the doctor to Liz Smith for verification). Even after the abortion, Kennedy still tried to continue the relationship, but she resisted.

Exner, who died of cancer in 1999, was vilified in the press for years, accused of compromising the Kennedy presidency and damaging "Camelot."

"I would not have got involved with Giancana and Roselli had Jack Kennedy not asked me," she told Liz Smith. Then she added:

"Before I die, I think the Camelot myth should ... be demystified, and the Kennedy legend examined for its reality."

Exner had been in a serious and long-term relationship with John Kennedy, where love was part of the equation. Marilyn Monroe was more of a conquest and strictly about sex.

Reports of when Kennedy and Monroe met vary. Some claim it was as early as the mid-1950s; FBI files say it was early in 1962 (though new evidence shows the FBI was wrong about this). What all the accounts do agree on is that Kennedy's wife, Jacqueline, very likely knew of the affair between her husband and Monroe, which is why she chose not to show up for Kennedy's birthday celebration in May 1962. That was the evening Monroe sang her now famous breathy version of "Happy Birthday" to her lover, the president of the United States.

About this time, however, John was actually trying to terminate the relationship. He sent his brother Robert to direct Monroe's attentions away from him. In the process, Robert promptly fell for Monroe himself. They had a torrid two-month affair during which time Robert shared a lot of information with Monroe, including the plot to kill Castro. Then suddenly, without warning, he shut her out cold.

Marilyn Monroe stands between Robert (left) and John F. Kennedy at a Democratic fundraising event in 1962.

From mid-July 1962 on, neither of the Kennedy brothers would take Monroe's phone calls. She was angry about the relationships ending, but far angrier about the way they had cut her off. She told someone she was tempted to hold a press conference to expose what had been going on. She didn't realize her house and phone were being bugged when she said this.

Besides the Kennedys, two other people had a lot to lose if Monroe's relationship with the brothers became public. Both Frank Sinatra and Sam Giancana were still close to the Kennedys at this time and felt they had much to gain by John remaining in power. Sam was also anxious to keep the Castro plot quiet.

A scheme was hatched to ensure Monroe was silenced.

Sinatra invited her to spend the weekend at the Cal-Neva Lodge on July 28 and 29, 1962. Paul D'Amato, who ran the lodge for Sinatra and Sam, told Anthony Summers, author of CONSPIRACY, his memories of the weekend:

"There was more to what happened than anyone has told. It would have been a big fall for Bobby Kennedy, wouldn't it?"

Monroe had not even wanted to go to the Cal-Neva that weekend, but finally agreed, partly to celebrate her new film deal with Fox and partly because Sinatra told her he wanted to discuss the film they were both going to be starring in, *What a Way to Go*. Sinatra, Sam, and Peter Lawford were the three men at the party. Various prostitutes were also reportedly there. Monroe's name never showed up on the lodge's register. According to Donald Wolfe, in his 1998 book, THE LAST DAYS OF MARILYN MONROE, she stayed in Bungalow 52, part of the area reserved for friends of Sinatra and Sam. At one point, she phoned her ex-husband Joe DiMaggio from there, but when he arrived at the lodge to see her, he was prevented from entering the premises on orders from Sinatra. And Monroe was, in effect, prevented from going out.

As Wolfe wrote, "Bellboys who delivered food to her room said that the door was usually answered by Peter Lawford and that they never saw her leave the room."

There was a good reason for that. Jimmy "Blue Eyes" Alo, business partner of organized crime figure Meyer Lansky, said he saw Monroe there with Sinatra and Lawford. They kept her drugged, he later recounted: "It was disgusting." Monroe's hosts then maneuvered her into a position where it appeared she had taken part in an orgy. Sinatra took photos, the results of which showed an incapacitated Monroe in several humiliating circumstances, one involving Sam. One of Sinatra's photographers told Gus Russo, author of THE OUTFIT, that a little while after that weekend, Sinatra had shown him proofs of photos he'd taken. The photographer was repulsed and recommended Sinatra destroy the photos. Sinatra reportedly agreed to do so.

On later tapes, FBI agent Roemer picked up parts of a conversation between Sam and Roselli discussing the Cal-Neva weekend. "You sure get your rocks off f—ing the same broad as the brothers, don't you," Roselli said to Sam.

It was some time before Roemer realized the "brothers" were the Kennedys.

Lawford, later questioned about what had gone on, claimed that Monroe's drugged state was the result of a suicide attempt because she was despondent over being fired by Fox. He knew better than anyone that she had just signed a new contract. This was only one of many cover-ups that weekend, but they paled in comparison with the cover-ups to come a week later, on the night Monroe died.

The truth of what happened in the late hours of August 4 and the early hours of August 5, 1962 will likely never be known. Marilyn Monroe died, but whether it was really by her own hand is still a question. Every effort was made to have the public believe that, and the initial story was that she committed suicide by ingesting an entire bottle of pills. But there was no pill residue in her stomach and no glass of water nearby with which she would have swallowed the pills. Who, then, killed her?

Sam eventually claimed that his people did it—using a Nembutal suppository—in order to frame Robert Kennedy, who was at Monroe's place early on the evening of August 4. However, as Sam told Chuck, the frame didn't work because when Marilyn's body was found, the Kennedys were informed and their people came in and cleaned everything up.

SENDING A MESSAGE

Between the many government senate committees looking into their activities and the FBI's relentless pursuit of them, U.S. mobsters were feeling the heat in the early 1960s. In all locations and in all cities where they had bugs, the FBI picked up the same message: The Mob felt betrayed by the Kennedys. They felt they had been double-crossed. They wanted revenge.

A 1962 FBI report of one conversation in which Sam and several colleagues took part read: "They discuss golf. Somebody asks if Bobby Kennedy plays golf; they know John Kennedy does. Suggest putting a bomb in his golf bag. (They all laugh.)"

A bug in 1963 picked up Santo Trafficante Jr. promising that Kennedy would get what's coming to him: "He is going to be hit."

Sam was particularly angry. "We got [Bobby] on the wire calling me a guinea greaseball ... can you believe that?" he asked Chuck. "My millions were good enough for 'em, weren't they? The votes I muscled for 'em were good enough to get Jack elected. So now I'm a f—ing greaseball, am I? Well, I'm gonna send them a message they'll never forget."

"The president is dead."

That was all Hoover said when Robert Kennedy answered the phone at 2.30 p.m. on November 22, 1963. This was a follow-up call to the one Robert had received two hours before telling him John had been shot. His first thought was that Sam Giancana was behind his brother's assassination. He was only partly right. Sam was not the only one involved. The crime organizations of Santo Trafficante Jr. and Carlos Marcello took part too. This was certainly not public knowledge at the time—Lee Harvey Oswald was almost immediately arrested—but some people did begin to put the pieces together. Bill Bonanno, a member of New York's Bonanno crime family, was one of these. When he saw Jack Ruby shoot Oswald two days after Kennedy's death, his suspicions were confirmed. "[Ruby] was out of Chicago and New Orleans," Bonanno later wrote in BOUND BY HONOR. "He belonged to Sam Giancana like a pinkie ring. He had been living in Texas for some time and had been running in our world for years. There could be no mistaking the meaning of his involvement."

Bonanno sent a lieutenant to Trafficante to find out what exactly had happened. The answer was clear. "His family was involved, along with Carlos Marcello's and Sam Giancana's," Bonanno wrote. "Jimmy Hoffa was involved too, but was not responsible for much."

If Bonanno needed further proof, he got it a few years later when he met up with Johnny Roselli in prison, where both men were incarcerated. Roselli had been disenchanted with Sam for some time, and he told Bonanno that he was especially upset with what had happened the day President Kennedy was shot.

"I was supposed to have a car waiting," began Roselli. "You think there was a car waiting? There was s— and I'm coming out of the sewer holding the f—ing piece in my hand. Sam and I both knew I was going to be the one to make the hit ... My position is in the storm drain ... There were four of us including the patsy [Oswald], but Sam and everyone else knew I was the one who'd have the shot ... I've just killed the f—ing president and there's no backup!"

That Roselli was so forthcoming surprised Bonanno. Why risk such a story coming out? And, if what Roselli said was true, Bonanno had questions: Why were the storm drains not sealed down by the Secret Service? Why were the windows in the depository open when the Secret Service would normally have them all locked up tight? How could Roselli have taken up his position in the storm drain and escaped Secret Service detection unless he had their co-operation? Bonanno decided he already had too much information. He didn't want to know more.

Neither did Chuck.

Shortly before Sam moved to Mexico in 1966, he and Chuck got together. Sam had just finished telling him that the Mob and the CIA had been partners on too many deals for him to even list them all. Seeing that Chuck didn't believe him, Sam fixed his brother with "a steely, impenetrable gaze" and intoned, "We took care of Kennedy ... together."

Sam added that the entire conspiracy went right to the top of the CIA, and he confirmed the involvement of the Trafficante and Marcello families. He also stated that Ruby had been called on to kill Oswald.

In his research for CONSPIRACY, Anthony Summers found a fragment of a rare television interview with Ruby, filmed during a recess at one of his court appearances. Ruby was asked if he thought the truth would ever come out.

"No," Ruby replied, adding:

"... because unfortunately these people, who have so much to gain and have such an ulterior motive to put me in the

position I'm in, will never let the true facts come above board to the world."

"I thought they'd get one of us, but Jack, after all he's been through, never worried about it," Robert Kennedy had said to a colleague only hours after his brother's assassination. "I thought it would be me."

"They" was the Mob and "they" eventually got Robert, too.

CHAPTER EIGHT
EXILE

8

Sam was really tired. He had told Chuck once that he thought the 1960s would be "my decade," but it hadn't turned out that way. Things had started off with such promise, with no less a possibility than that of having a president in his back pocket. That mission had failed, and even seeing the Kennedys pay for their betrayal—to him and mobsters everywhere—gave him little satisfaction. Now it was January 16, 1964, and as he looked down at the story in that day's *Chicago Tribune*, Sam wondered how it had all gone wrong.

"Inside Story of Meeting to Fire Giancana," the headline screamed. According to the paper, a meeting had taken place in December to discuss Sam's future. It was presided over by Accardo and Ricca and included six other top "hoodlums": Sam "Teets" Battaglia, William "Potatoes" Daddano, Felix "Milwaukee Phil" Alderisio, Rudolph Fratta, Frank "One Ear" Fratta, and Albert "Obbie" Frabotta.

The problems had been building for years. Yes, Sam knew he had made a few mistakes during that time, but he didn't understand why Accardo and Ricca were so upset with him. As far as he was concerned, things only started going off the rails when the Kennedys and the FBI began to turn up the heat on organized crime.

Talking to the press, Sam saw, had been one big mistake. The first time he'd done that was at Antoinette's wedding early in 1959. Sandy Smith, a *Chicago Tribune* reporter, got the first interview Sam had ever given to the media. It was triggered when Sam caught Smith and other reporters looking at place cards for the wedding guests. The names on the cards read like a Who's Who of the Chicago Mob and Smith was writing them all down. At first angry, Sam later came round, and talked to Smith openly about many subjects.

"I'd like to tell them to go to hell, but I guess I'll keep my mouth shut and take the Fifth Amendment," he said when asked what he would say at his upcoming appearance before the Senate's McClellan Committee. He also bemoaned the lot of ex-convicts who couldn't get a break. Pointing to his new son-in-law, Sam proclaimed, "Now everybody is going to hook him up with me. No one will hire him. I'll have to give him a .45 and put him to work for me."

One could imagine Accardo's displeasure at reading *that* in the paper, but it was another statement from Sam that would upset Accardo even more.

"What's wrong with the Syndicate?" Sam asked Smith. "Two or three of us get together on some deal and everybody says it's a bad thing, but those businessmen do it all the time and nobody squawks."

Until that moment no one in the Mob had ever publicly admitted the Syndicate existed.

Things did not improve a few months later when Sam committed another huge error on his return from Mexico, where he'd gone to negotiate the purchase of a racetrack. When the FBI learned of his whereabouts, they alerted U.S. Customs, who made a point of meeting and searching him when he re-entered the country. He was found to have a list on him that, although in code, named most of the top-ranked members of the Outfit. Beside each name was a number. As agent Roemer later said, the numbers referred to the percentage that each person on the list would own of the racetrack. In addition to men such as Accardo and Humphreys, three First Ward politicians were also named. They included Alderman John D'Arco, who, not surprisingly, had grown up in the Patch. A couple of months after this revelation, D'Arco conveniently had a heart attack and announced he would not be seeking re-election.

Sam stepped in to pick D'Arco's replacement to run for alderman, but his choice brought further embarrassment to the Outfit. Sam decided that his nephew, State Senator Anthony DeTolve, would be a perfect fit, provided he kept his head low and stayed out of the spotlight. The election was a shoe-in, Sam figured, because "it ain't like there's going to be a real election here." Unfortunately, DeTolve kept such a low profile the press could not find him. They resorted to ridiculing him until he was finally forced to talk to a reporter.

"Let's get one thing straight," DeTolve was quoted as saying. "I haven't been hiding. I'm just busy, all the time busy."

That's all the press needed to dub the candidate Anthony "Busy-Busy" DeTolve. The papers annihilated him, scuttling any hopes he had of being elected. Sam realized DeTolve had to go, even though the election was just days away. The precinct captains were told to instruct voters to write in Michael Fio Rito as candidate. Fio Rito won by an overwhelming majority, but was forced to resign after 19 days when it was discovered he was not actually a ward resident. The office sat vacant for some time before another Mob-backed politician could be found to take the post. The whole episode suggested that Sam was losing his touch.

The McGuire Sisters, (left to right), Christine, Dorothy and Phyllis, sit with Sam Giancana and hairdresser Frederic Jones after their performance at a London nightclub in 1961.

And then there were his legendary run-ins with FBI agent Roemer. The loudest one occurred in July 1961 at Chicago's O'Hare airport and involved Sam's long-time paramour, Phyllis McGuire. Accardo liked members of the Outfit to maintain a low profile and Sam hadn't done much of that in recent years. He'd been seen everywhere with McGuire, who, with her sisters, was at the top of her singing fame at that time. The FBI had been leaving the relationship alone, but decided on this occasion to use it to put pressure on Sam. They met the two at O'Hare and managed to spirit McGuire away for an interview without Sam knowing. When he found out, Sam had a lengthy and heated exchange with Roemer, part of which went:

Sam: "I suppose you intend to report this [meeting] to your boss!"

Roemer: "Who's my boss?"

Sam: "J. Edgar Hoover."

Roemer: "Yes, I imagine he'll see a copy."

Sam: "F— J. Edgar Hoover and your super boss!"

Roemer: "Who is that?"

Sam: "Bobby Kennedy."

Roemer: "Might be he'll see a copy, yes."

Sam: "F— Bobby Kennedy and your super, super boss!"

Roemer: "Who is my super, super boss?"

Sam: "John Kennedy!"

Roemer: "I doubt the president of the United States is interested in Sam Giancana."

Sam: "F— John Kennedy. Listen Roemer, I know all about the Kennedys, and Phyllis knows more about the Kennedys and one of these days we're going to tell all."

Roemer: "What are you talking about?"

Sam: "F— you. One of these days it'll come out. You wait, you smart a—, you'll see."

They continued to trade insults back and forth, and then Roemer realized they were drawing quite a bit of attention.

"All you folks come over here!" he yelled at the growing crowd of onlookers. "Take a look at this piece of slime! This is Sam Giancana! He is the boss of the underworld here in Chicago! Take a good look at this garbage!"

Another agent finally intervened to calm Roemer down, but it was clear that Sam had brought negative attention to himself and the Mob in a very public place. Word quickly got back to Accardo about him losing his cool yet again.

A similar event two years later spelled doom for Sam. Roemer and agent Marshall Rutland were tailing Sam, who was riding in a car with Chuckie English. They all pulled up to the Armory Lounge and the agents followed their marks inside before realizing they were on Sam's home turf. Roemer and Rutland were suddenly surrounded by angry patrons telling them to leave Sam alone. Things finally settled down and the agents stayed for a drink. As they left later, English came running after Roemer.

"Sam wants to give you a message. He says if Kennedy wants to talk to him, he knows who to go through."

"Sounds like he's talking about Frank Sinatra," Roemer said.

"You said it," English replied.

When Humphreys was told about this conversation, he exploded.

"For C— sakes, that's a cardinal rule!" Humphreys shouted. "You don't give up a legit guy! He tells Roemer that Sinatra is our guy to Kennedy?"

It was one more strike against Sam, by this time a man walking on thin ice. Staying out of the limelight was just not his style.

Sam didn't feel he was to blame for any of what had started to go wrong for the Mob, but as he looked down at the newspaper on that January day in 1964, even he had to acknowledge he was in trouble.

"Giancana's behavior as a playboy paying court to a night club singer, his legal quarrels with the [FBI], and his temper have brought far too much publicity to a mob which now prefers to function behind the façade of legitimate business," the *Chicago Tribune* story stated. It also reported that the decision had been made at the meeting to demote Sam, although Accardo and Ricca still had to have this move approved "by the national brotherhood of crime," which was the Commission.

What Sam did after he saw the 1964 newspaper article is not known, but he must have put his survival skills to good use because he managed to remain as head of the Outfit for more than another year. When New York crime boss Joseph Bonanno disappeared in October 1964, suspicion quickly fell on Sam because the two of them had been feuding. Even after it became clear Sam wasn't responsible, some observers feared that a gang war was brewing. (Bonanno eventually reappeared in May 1966, amid accusations that he had staged his own kidnapping.)

Bonanno's abduction was the least of Sam's worries, however, as the Outfit's revenues declined and FBI surveillance rose. The top brass at the Outfit wanted Sam to stay in Chicago and look after matters there, but he wasn't used to taking orders. Nevertheless, at a meeting at the end of October 1964, he agreed that an operating director could be named to run the Outfit during his absences. If Sam could see his power slowly eroding, he chose to ignore this reality and carried on globetrotting.

In 1965, the FBI took a different tack to get at Sam. They convened a Grand Jury investigation into, among other things, bribery of federal officials and the use of violence in interstate commerce. But their main goal was to trap Sam into finally talking. Federal prosecutors achieved this by granting him immunity from prosecution. Sam therefore couldn't plead the Fifth Amendment because he couldn't be prosecuted for anything he had to say about himself. Still, even with this immunity, Sam would not betray his own set of rules. He was determined to remain faithful to *omertà* even if it meant going to prison.

The court paraded an endless stream of Mob witnesses in front of the Grand Jury and laid out extensive evidence of their transgressions. Much of the evidence had been collected from the FBI's illegal wiretaps. Sam was becoming unnerved, but the appearance of Phyllis McGuire sent him over the edge. He was sure she was selling him out and it played right into the FBI's plans. After McGuire's first day of testimony, Sam was livid at the perceived betrayal. In a city lounge that evening, an FBI agent witnessed Sam's eruption. The Don author William Brashler quotes the agent as saying of the scene:

"[Giancana] saved his choicest rancor for Phyllis McGuire, finally standing and shouting a string of obscenities in which he claimed that although he had lavishly romanced her throughout the years, she was now turning on him. He bellowed, 'I'm getting f—ed!'"

Sam Giancana in custody in 1965, after he was ordered to jail for refusing to answer the questions of a federal Grand Jury investigating his activities.

Despite his outburst, Sam held his cool in court on June 1, 1965, and answered only the first two questions put to him: what was his name and where did he live. After that he refused to speak. This got him sent to prison on contempt charges for the term of the Grand Jury—a year. While Sam was in prison, Sam Battaglia stepped in to run things at the Outfit, under the supervision of Ricca and Accardo, who were never far away.

As Sam's date for release approached, there were discussions by federal officials about going through the court process again to keep Sam in prison for another year. But the wily kid from the Patch still had some pull with the CIA and he was able to avoid the extended sentence.

Shortly after his release, Sam met with Ricca and Accardo. Ricca had always been his biggest supporter, but even he agreed that Sam should be stripped of whatever remaining power he had and told to leave the country. Angry, Sam nevertheless agreed to go and chose to take Richard Cain with him. Cain—a discredited policeman, then private detective, and finally conman and hoodlum—had also grown up in the Patch, but in the generation after Sam. He'd been working with the Mob for years. Cain's ability to speak Spanish was one of the main reasons Sam picked him, since he'd decided to make Mexico his new home. By the fall of 1966, the two men had relocated and started setting up another Giancana empire.

The years of being followed and harassed had left Sam paranoid about secrecy, so in Mexico he adopted (unofficially) the name of Riccardo Scalzetti (in truth, Richard Cain's birth name). Most of Sam's social contacts in Mexico had no idea who he was until Sandy Smith did a *Life* magazine exposé on him and blew his cover.

Sam settled more or less into his life in exile. Only once, in July 1968, did he slip back into the States after learning that the front window of his daughter Bonnie's house had been blown out with a shotgun blast. She and her family were unhurt. Another mobster's house was hit not long after that, and then a small bomb exploded in Bonanno's backyard (Bonanno was now home after his abduction). The talk of a gang war persisted with each new incident—until three men were arrested a year later for the crimes and found to have been hired for their efforts by David Hale, a special agent for the FBI. Hale resigned, but refused to testify about the bombings and was never prosecuted.

Cain traveled back and forth between the United States and Mexico, taking care of affairs for Sam. At one point he had to leave Sam for three years when he was arrested during a visit to the States and convicted on an old charge. He returned to Mexico in 1971, but the relationship between him and Sam was becoming strained. Sam was winding down his activities and felt content to live on what he'd already set up. Cain, on the other hand, was eager to get some new ventures going and he was promoting one in particular with which Sam didn't want any involvement. Cain persisted.

Sam had had enough. The now gray-haired hood may have lost his power, but it seems a few shreds of influence remained. The Mob back home warned Cain not to proceed with his plans, but he wouldn't listen. A few days before Christmas 1973, in Rose's Sandwich Shop in an old Sicilian neighborhood of Chicago, Cain was gunned down. Despite Sam reaching out to his old cohorts, however, the actual hit on Cain was reportedly not one that he had ordered.

Even though his health was deteriorating rapidly throughout 1974, Sam did not give any thought to returning to Chicago. He was convinced that if he did, the government would be there waiting to arrest him. He was not far wrong.

CHAPTER NINE
SAUSAGES AND DEATH

It was July 18, 1974, and the Mexican summer evening was warm. Sam, dressed only in a bathrobe and slippers, puttered about in his walled garden, tending to his plants. The 66-year-old had not been in good health for some time. Stomach and abdominal problems often gave him intense pain. This made him irritable with everyone and kept his traveling to a minimum. However, his empire was in good hands, so he spent much of his time at his estate, called San Cristóbal, in the La Quintas section of Cuernavaca, or, when his health allowed it, on the golf course.

Sam had no plans of ever leaving Mexico, although he'd given up trying to become a legal resident. For eight years, he had been a non-resident alien and, thanks to the greasing of many palms, seemed safe from deportation. What he didn't know was that the United States was putting pressure on Mexico to throw him out of the country and back onto

American soil. So, as he shuffled about the garden that evening in bathrobe and slippers, the stub of a cigar in his hand, he didn't see what was coming. Two men suddenly appeared, grabbed him, and dragged him to a waiting car.

The men forcing him into the vehicle were Mexican and when Sam realized they were immigration officials, he erupted in a fury. This was not supposed to happen. Jorge Castillo was supposed to keep things under control. Castillo was a well-established lawyer in Mexico with strong political ties. He was especially close to Luis Echeverría, then president of Mexico. Sam had millions of dollars tied up in the country, which was now the base for his operations. Through Castillo, he had connections right up to Echeverría to ensure his status as non-resident alien continued. Something had gone horribly wrong.

Sam quickly discovered that he was totally on his own. When Castillo found out that Sam was being deported, the lawyer himself quietly left the country, too.

In spite of his shouting and threats, Sam was held in jail overnight without courtesy of a phone call. The United States Consulate in Mexico City had been phoned to verify Sam's American citizenship. This had set off a chain of events as lawmen scrambled to prepare for the gangster's return to the U.S. His deportation was formally arranged. The next morning, he was handed a rumpled blue shirt and a pair of beltless cotton pants a few sizes too big and put on a plane bound for San Antonio, Texas. In exiting the country, Sam left behind not only his properties, but—in keeping with local law—the millions of dollars he'd deposited in Mexican banks.

The FBI now had to move quickly so that Sam wouldn't slip through their fingers and disappear. In short order, San Antonio agents served Sam with a subpoena to appear before a Chicago Grand Jury the following week. On arrival in Texas, the wily old mobster claimed he couldn't afford to go to Chicago because he'd been thrown out of Mexico without a cent and had nothing but the clothes on his back. The FBI picked up the cost of his air fare.

When Sam got off the plane in Chicago, he was still wearing his slippers and had his bathrobe draped over one arm. He used both hands to hold up his over-sized pants. The FBI's William Roemer was taken aback at the sight of his old adversary at the airport. He'd rushed there hoping to have it out again with Sam, but he almost didn't recognize the scraggly bearded and considerably aged man.

"He was undoubtedly the wealthiest person on that plane, but he looked like some Italian immigrant landing at Ellis Island, destitute and frail," recalled Roemer. And if he was expecting a fight with the once-mighty Sam Giancana, he was disappointed. Sam made it very clear things had changed.

"I'm not gonna be involved in anything anymore," he told Roemer. "You'll soon find out that I have nothin' goin' for me here, I'm out of it. So, please, just leave me alone. Nothin' personal like it was between us before. If it takes an apology, then this is it. Let's just forget what has been before." Roemer backed down.

The Chicago police took Sam downtown for questioning and, just like old times, the press waited to snap photos. But things really had changed because Sam was now far out of touch with the day-to-day goings-on of the Outfit. The police asked him about his movements, friends, and businesses, but—as usual—got few answers. They then moved on to direct questions about the murder of Richard Cain. Sam told them he knew nothing about it and wasn't even in the country when it happened. After there was nothing left to ask, Sam was allowed to go back to his Oak Park home, which had been looked after in the years of his absence by his caretaker, Joe DiPersio, and Joe's wife.

Sam spent the next few weeks settling back into a routine of sorts. So did the FBI, who resumed watching his house and following him around. Because he no longer had the Armory Lounge, he conducted business from phone booths and corner restaurants. Dominick "Butch" Blasi—one of Sam's former lieutenants—was now working for Joey "Doves" Aiuppa, the Mob's operating boss in Chicago, but he was still close to Sam and spent a great deal of time chauffeuring him around. They would leave Oak Park in the morning, with Sam waving to the FBI agents on his way out, and Blasi would stop at various phone booths around town to allow Sam to make his calls and set up his meetings. Many of these meetings took place on the golf course when Sam was up to it.

Despite his comments to Roemer, Sam couldn't help wanting to establish himself again within the Outfit. He tried to find a place in the old guard to fit into, but no place was left. Sam's time had come and gone—only he didn't see by how much. He was no longer in the game, but he still insisted on coming up to bat.

Tony Accardo still held tight control of Chicago and there was no way he was going back to a time when Sam had brought endless FBI and police attention to every member of the Mob. Accardo hoped Sam would realize that most of the old guard were dead and times had changed. The Mob had managed to turn down the spotlight on the Outfit's activities since Sam had left for Mexico—and, if Accardo could help it, they were going to keep it that way.

Strike one.

Sam did have one thing they wanted, though, and that was a very lucrative gambling operation in the Caribbean, including five gambling boats that turned huge profits. During the latter years of Sam's reign in Chicago, the Outfit's revenues had declined considerably, a trend that had worsened in the past eight years. So, while letting Sam back on board wasn't in Accardo's plans, getting at his money was. Accardo started by simply telling Sam that they were entitled to some of the profits from his gambling ventures. Sam was having no part of that and told Accardo so. The gambling businesses, he said, had been set up by him after he left for Mexico; they had nothing to do with Chicago. The only two Outfit members with any connection to his operations, Blasi and Gus Alex, were paid a small share by him. No one else had any claim on it as far as Sam was concerned.

Strike two.

The week after his arrival back in Chicago, Sam had appeared before the Grand Jury as requested, and this time he talked—though he managed to say absolutely nothing. Between July 1974 and February 1975, he appeared before the Grand Jury four times.

Then in May 1975, while in California with a new girlfriend, Sam suffered a pain in his stomach unlike any before. He ended up undergoing gall bladder surgery in Houston. Three weeks later he returned to Chicago, but suffered a relapse that sent him back to Houston for more treatment. Finally, on June 18, he returned once more to Chicago and was met at the airport by Blasi. He climbed slowly and gingerly into the car that took him home.

The next day, June 19, members of the Senate Committee to Study Governmental Operations with Respect to Intelligence Activities were scheduled to arrive in Chicago too. Sam was under subpoena to appear before them a couple of days later. Some members of the Mob were nervous about what he might say, but not necessarily around the issue of the CIA–Mob plot to assassinate Castro. That had, by then, become more or less public knowledge. Johnny Roselli was due to testify about it a week after Sam and, even though it was known he was going to be forthcoming, no one had knocked him off. That seemed to be a good sign that Sam wasn't in danger if he spoke as well.

However, there was another group besides the Mob with a greater reason to fear that Sam might crack: the CIA. *Omertà* ran too strongly through his veins to be a true threat to the Outfit in terms of revealed secrets, but the CIA could not be sure about Sam's allegiance to it. By now it was known that the Mob and the CIA had been involved in an assassination plot against Castro. But what was still unclear (and has never been confirmed to this day) was whether the CIA was involved in the plot to assassinate President Kennedy. (A year later, Roselli, due to testify once more and increasingly loose with talk about both the Castro and Kennedy assassination plots, suddenly disappeared. He was later found in an oil can, dead and dismembered, in Trafficante's home base in Florida.)

But Sam would not be around to hear that news. In mid-1975 he was too busy being vocal about not wanting to "rot in jail" —and many people did not want to hear that from him.

Strike three.

THE LAST SUPPER

It seems surprising that an old mobster like Sam wouldn't realize that even close friends—especially in a business like his—might not be trustworthy. Sam of all people should have known that.

June 19, 1975, was an unusually hot summer day and Sam spent most of it just resting after his recent health scares. Chuck English came over in the afternoon and the two sat around talking until 7 p.m., when they were joined by Sam's youngest daughter, Francine, and her family and by Butch Blasi. Since Sam had had his gall bladder removed, some forbidden foods could now be added back into his diet. Knowing this, Francine had brought him his favorite sausages, *escarole* (endive), and *ceci* beans. He was saving them for later. The group ate an informal dinner together and then sat around talking until English and Blasi left to go home. This was recorded by the team of Chicago detectives keeping surveillance on the house. Then at 10 p.m. Francine and the others left Sam. They weren't far from the house when they saw Blasi coming toward them on the road, and they nodded to each other as their cars passed. The detectives duly noted that Blasi pulled into Sam's driveway and walked into the house.

It was a random watch not only on Sam's house, but on those of other mobsters living in the area. The detectives never stayed at one residence for long. On this night, after Blasi's return, they left to check out both the Chuckie English and Tony Accardo residences before returning to Sam's house.

The last time Joe DiPersio saw Sam that evening he had been wearing a blue-and-white checked sports shirt, brown pants, and his usual black house slippers. DiPersio called down from upstairs at about 10.30 p.m. to ask if Sam wanted anything. Sam said no, but that he'd call him if needed. DiPersio closed his bedroom door and settled down to watch the *Tonight Show*.

It had been a long time since Sam was able to enjoy his favorite meal. In one pan he boiled up the *escarole* and *ceci* beans and he cooked the sausage in another. When they were all done he began to sauté the *escarole* and beans in the sausage grease, intending to share this popular snack from the Old Country with his friend. They were in the basement kitchen, off the dining room area. There was a steel door leading to the backyard, but on this hot summer night it was closed to keep the air conditioning operating smoothly.

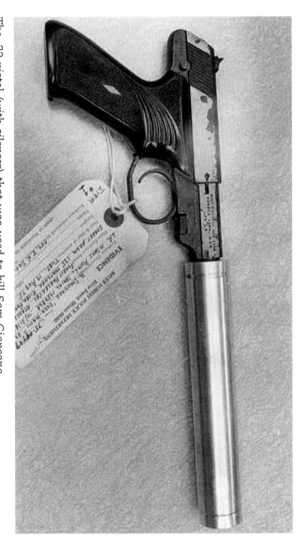

The .22 pistol (with silencer) that was used to kill Sam Giancana.

Sam felt safer here than anywhere else and, with his back to his friend, chatted as he cooked. But the person he'd known for so many years wasn't thinking about food: his mind was on the job he'd been ordered to do. The police later said that a .22 caliber pistol was an unusual weapon for a Mob hit. It was obviously chosen because, even with the silencer attached, it was a smaller gun than the more common Mob weapon. The killer needed something easy to hide from his victim.

Whether Sam had a split second of feeling the gun at the back of his head will never be known, but as he cooked his last meal—one that he'd never get to eat—the trigger was pulled and a bullet entered the back of his neck and lodged in the front-left portion of his brain. He fell with a thud, landing flat on his back. The killer reached down quickly and put the muzzle of the silencer into Sam's mouth and shot again. Then he put the gun under Sam's chin and fired five more bullets. His final act was to rifle through the dead man's pockets and wallet, after which he threw the wallet (still containing $1,400) five feet away from the body. He left through the steel door. As the assassin was driving away through the upper section of Oak Park and into River Forest, police cars came roaring toward him on a totally unrelated call. The killer couldn't know this, so he turned onto Thatcher Road, pulled over, and tossed the gun out the window.

At 11 p.m. DiPersio called down to his boss one more time to see if he needed anything, but this time he got no reply. He went downstairs where he found Sam's bloodied body.

"I was so shocked when I went down there and saw him," DiPersio later told Antoinette Giancana.

"I said 'Mooney, what happened?' He was like a brother. We'd been together for thirty-one years. I couldn't believe he was dead."

The food was still cooking and had not yet burned, so the killer was not long gone. DiPersio turned off the gas stove and phoned the family, an ambulance, and then the police.

Sam's estate was officially valued at only $132,583.16. Listed among the itemized inventory of his possessions was a small hinged globe engraved: "Poor Sam—the World Is Yours."

A few months later, the murder weapon was discovered where it had been thrown on Thatcher Road—coincidentally on the way from Oak Park to the home of Blasi. Gus Russo wrote in THE OUTFIT that in 2001 a source close to Blasi claimed that Blasi even admitted to having been the perpetrator.

In the 2003 book Double Deal, the authors—Sam Giancana (Sam's nephew and namesake) and Michael Corbitt (disgraced ex-cop and long-time Mob employee)—say firmly that the killer was Mob member Tony Spilotro. During a conversation with mobster Sal Bastone, Corbitt learned that Spilotro lived near Sam and often visited him, even finding a back way in through people's yards so that he could not be seen. Spilotro had been a big favorite of Sam's, and the latter had helped the younger man move up through the Mob. According to Sam's nephew and Corbitt, Sam would not open the door to just anyone. The two men ruled out both Blasi and English.

"Yeah, Sam and Butch were real close," Bastone told Corbitt. "And the same thing with him and Chuckie. Besides, neither one of them had the balls to do somethin' like that. There's only one guy that had the balls to do Sam."

"Sal didn't have to say the name," Corbitt wrote. "I knew he was talking about Tony Spilotro."

In the end, it didn't really matter who had murdered Sam. Death by violence was inevitable. In truth, it was amazing that the kid from the Patch had defied the odds, first of his childhood and then his line of work, to stay alive as long as he did. Although she brought down anger on herself from her children and her siblings, his daughter Antoinette stated the picture clearly in a conversation with television newsman Bill Kurtis the day after the murder:

"You know, Bill, the way you live is the way you die. Sam lived by the gun, so he died by the gun."

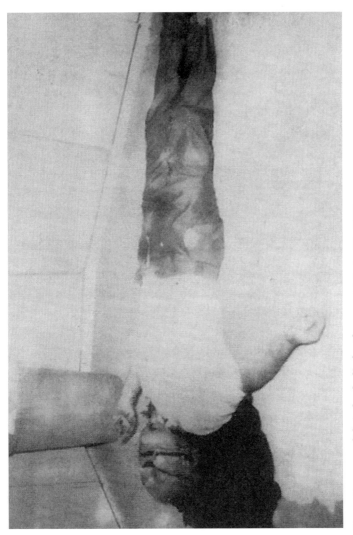

Sam Giancana did, indeed, die by the gun on June 19, 1975.

FURTHER READING

Bill Bonanno. BOUND BY HONOR. New York, USA: St. Martin's Press, 1999.

William Brashler. THE DON. New York, USA: Harper & Row, 1977.

Antoinette Giancana & Thomas C. Renner. MAFIA PRINCESS. New York, USA: Morrow, 1984.

Sam & Chuck Giancana. DOUBLE CROSS. New York, USA: Warner Books, 1992.

Seymour M. Hersh. THE DARK SIDE OF CAMELOT. Boston, MA: Little, Brown, 1997.

Thomas A. Reppetto. AMERICAN MAFIA. New York, USA: H. Holt, 2004.

William F. Roemer. MAN AGAINST THE MOB. New York, USA: Ballantine Books, 1989.

Gus Russo. THE OUTFIT. New York, USA: Bloomsbury, 2001.

David E. Scheim. CONTRACT ON AMERICA. New York, USA: Shopolsky Publishers Inc., 1988.

Anthony Summers. CONSPIRACY. New York, USA: McGraw-Hill, 1980.

Donald. H. Wolfe. THE LAST DAYS OF MARILYN MONROE. New York, USA: Morrow, 1998.

INDEX